REPORT 2004

A MAN'S GUIDE TO WOMEN

PLEASURE PRINCIPLES, SECRET SEDUCTIONS,
AND HIDDEN TECHNIQUES TO MAKE YOU THE MAN
SHE DREAMS ABOUT

RODALE

RODALE

WE **INSPIRE** AND **ENABLE** PEOPLE TO IMPROVE
THEIR LIVES AND THE WORLD AROUND THEM

FOR MORE OF OUR PRODUCTS
www.RODALESTORE.com
(800) 848-4735

Sex and Values at Rodale

We believe that an active and healthy sex life, based on mutual consent and respect between partners, is an important component of physical and mental well-being. We also respect that sex is a private matter and that each person has a different opinion of what sexual practices or levels of discourse are appropriate. Rodale is committed to offering responsible, practical advice about sexual matters, supported by accredited professionals and legitimate scientific research. Our goal—for sex and all other topics—is to publish information that empowers people's lives.

Report 2004: A Man's Guide to Women Staff

Executive Editor: Jeremy Katz
Editor: Daniel Listwa
Contributing Writers: Don Alessi Jr., Matthew Barbour, Nicole
  Beland, Brian Boyé, Shannon Davis, Andy Ellis, Rebecca Gardyn,
  Ron Geraci, Brian Good, Kristina Grish, Lisa Jones, Joe Kita, Chris
  Lawson, Michael Lewittes, Matt Marion, Sarah Miller, Hugh
  O'Neill, Amy Sohn, Ted Spiker, Laurence Roy Stains, Bill Stieg,
  Alix Strauss, Lauren Weisberger, Mike Zimmerman
Interior and Cover Designer: Joanna Williams
Photo Editor: Natalie McGill
Research Editor: Bernadette M. Sukley
Project Editor: Kathryn C. LeSage
Copy Editors: Jennifer Hornsby, Caryn Radick
Layout Designer: Faith Hague
Product Specialist: Jodi Schaffer
Senior Managing Editor: Chris Krogermeier
Content Assembly Manager: Robert V. Anderson Jr.
Associate Content Assembly Manager: Patricia Brown
Vice President, Art Director: Andy Carpenter
Managing Art Director: Darlene Schneck
Vice President, Publisher, Direct Response Books: Gregg Michaelson
Senior Director, Direct Response Marketing: Janine Slaughter
Product Manager: Matthew Neumaier

CONTENTS

INTRODUCTION

Let's start with some basic math.

144.5 million = the number of women in North America

138.3 million = the number of men

1 = the number of women a guy needs to keep him sexually satisfied for life

I can already hear you laughing—especially you married guys in the back. After all, if a lifetime of super sex were truly as simple as 1 man + 1 woman, every guy who's currently in a relationship would be 100 percent sexually satisfied, 365 days a year.

So simple numbers don't tell the whole story (an important thing to remember the next time you find yourself lusting after a 36-24-36 figure). In truth, sexual satisfaction over the long haul is more like advanced calculus: You could work for years on one problem, but without a range of insights, you'll never get the right answer.

Of course, you want the right answers now. That's where *A Man's Guide to Women* can help. In your hand is a supercharged sex cheat sheet, with secrets and tips you'll count on for the rest of your life. Like these for example:

- **The secrets of the female mind, revealed.** Want to know what the blonde across the room is thinking about? Turn to page 88 to find out.
- **Our Sexual Aptitude Test.** This multiple-choice quiz will tell you, once and for all, what your sexual shortcomings are—and how to fix them.
- **The clothes she'll want to take off . . . of you.** Clothes don't just make the man; they also make the woman happy.
- **How to get her red hot with blue movies.** Porno, that is. Find out how to serve it up right, compliments of the female

adult film director whose flicks are just as popular with women as with men.

• **The blueprints for becoming a perfect husband.** It's not as bad as you think. Go to page 142 to learn how one guy solved the marriage puzzle.

• **How to date a younger woman.** For many men, the fountain of youth is no fantasy; it's a 20-something woman. Want to be one of those guys? You can.

I could keep going, but why bother. As you already know, it's not quantity that counts; it's quality.

Happy reading and good luck.

—Daniel Listwa
    Editor

1

IN SHAPE TO SCORE

Athletes—the faithful ones, at least—must have happy wives. After all, one of the perks of being in top physical form on the field is being in top form in the bedroom as well.

Luckily, you don't need to be an uber-jock to win a spot in her hall of fame. All you need is a little training and a little focus. We want you to be a sexual decathlete, ready for whatever games you'll play. Today, maybe it's a 2-minute sprint. Tonight, a marathon. And tomorrow, some pole-vaulting that'll really raise the bar on future events.

Consider this section your training manual: everything you need to know to go longer, faster, harder, and—most important—better than you've ever gone before. Practice, and we guarantee your gym won't be the only spot in the house that gets heavy use.

10 Things That Don't Matter in Bed

BY LISA JONES

1. Your penis. I care that you have one and that it functions properly; specs are irrelevant.

2. Exactly where your hands are . . . as long as they are always someplace on my skin.

3. What your previous girlfriend liked. I'm not her. For example, I would much prefer that you first suck on my nipples before you pinch them and then blow in my ear and kiss slowly down my body starting at my left clavicle—not the reverse order. See the difference?

4. What I liked last time.

5. That you can't get it up. Use your hands. Use your tongue. Just use something.

6. That I didn't orgasm this time. As long as you're willing to keep swinging for the bleachers, I can take one for the team.

7. Simultaneous orgasm. It's overrated. Frankly, if you're making me climax, I don't really care how, where, or when it happens.

8. Length of intercourse. If you're more of a sprinter than a distance runner, show me how good you are in the warmup (that would be the oral warmup).

9. Your baldness, beer belly, or love handles. If I cared about any of that, I wouldn't be in bed with you in the first place.

10. My choice of underwear. It's what's underneath that counts.

The Sex-for-Life Diet

Spicing up your sex life is simple: Just eat

BY BRIAN GOOD

THE PIECE YOU'RE ABOUT TO READ is based on the simple notion that (a) men like food and (b) men like sex, so (c) wouldn't it be great if you could actually eat your way to more fun in the bedroom?

Grunt if you agree.

Or maybe just sharpen your knife and fork. With help from nutritionists and the latest research, we've discovered 10 superfoods that can help you at every age and stage of your sex life—whether it's seducing women in your 20s, producing Mini-Me's in your 30s, or inducing your equipment to keep working in your 40s and beyond.

"Whether you've got a stamina-busting deficiency, clogged arteries that are limiting bloodflow, or a problem producing high-quality sperm, some simple changes to your diet could help alleviate the condition," says Elizabeth Ward, R.D., a Boston-based nutrition consultant. Meaning: Tweak your diet today and you could be having the best sex of your life tomorrow . . . and every day for the rest of your life.

YOUR 20S: MORE SEX, MORE STAYING POWER

THE FOOD: EGGS

THE BENEFIT: BE A LESS EXCITABLE BOY

It's your third date with the J.Lo look-alike from the Laundromat, and the anxiety's high. Will she come back to your place for the spin cycle? To calm your nerves, not to mention other body parts when you hit the bedroom, try taking things easy—or over easy, with a plateful of eggs on the morning of your big date. Scrambled, poached, or hard-boiled, eggs are a good source of B vitamins, a key nutrient for keeping your sex drive roaring and your mind stress-free. "Whenever you're feeling anxious, jittery, or stressed out, B vitamins are the first thing your body runs out of," says Paul Lachance, Ph.D., director of the Nutraceutical Institute at Rutgers University, New Jersey. Keep your levels high and your body will laugh at stress, helping you stay calmer in the bedroom and reducing your risk of performance anxiety and premature ejaculation.

THE FOOD: CELERY

THE BENEFIT: STOP STALKING, START SEDUCING

It's stringy and tastes like crunchy water, but celery is the swizzle stick that can stir up your sex life. Every stalk of the stuff is packed with androstenone and androstenol, two pheromones that can help you attract women the way trailer parks attract tornadoes. (Don't worry, these steroids are different from the steroid androstenedione.) "When you chew a stalk of celery, you release androstenone and androstenol odor molecules into your mouth. They then travel up the back of your throat to your nose," says Alan Hirsch, M.D., author of *Scentsational Sex.* "Once there, the pheromones boost your arousal, turning you on and causing your body to send off scents and signals that make you more desirable to women."

Try it the next time you're in a bar. Grab the celery from your brother-in-law's Bloody Mary and munch away. "The pheromones take effect immediately, so you should notice the women around you paying more attention to you right away," says Dr. Hirsch. And if you strike out? "Celery is a low-calorie, high-fiber food, so you can eat as much as you want and not regret it later," says Ward.

THE FOOD: VANILLA ICE CREAM

THE BENEFIT: BOWL HER OVER WITH YOUR ENDURANCE

When it comes to sex, ice cream is endurance food: It has high levels of calcium and phosphorus, two minerals that build your muscles' energy reserves and boost your libido. All that calcium (200 milligrams in the typical bowl) can also make your orgasms more powerful, since the muscles that control ejaculation need calcium in order to spasm and contract properly, says Sarah Brewer, M.B., author of *Increase Your Sex Drive*. Just choose vanilla over Cherry Garcia. A study conducted at Chicago's Smell and Taste Treatment and Research Foundation found that when men smell the scent of vanilla, it relaxes them, reducing anxiety and inhibitions. (Break out the Incredible Hulk costume!)

YOUR 30S: SEX WITH A PURPOSE

THE FOOD: BRAZIL NUTS

THE BENEFIT: SHAPE UP YOUR SWIMMERS

Cigarette smoke, air pollution, and other toxins in the air can damage your sperm, altering the DNA inside your cells and possibly increasing your child's risk of birth defects. Your best bet for fighting these pollutants? Call in the Brazilians. Brazil nuts are a top source of selenium, a vitamin that helps keep sperm cells healthy while also helping the little buggers swim faster. When researchers in the United Kingdom had men with fertility problems increase their selenium intake, the men produced hardier, more viable sperm cells. "Brazil nuts are also a good source of vitamin E, an antioxidant that helps protect sperm cells against free-radical damage," says Keith Ayoob, R.D., a spokesman for the American Dietetic Association.

INSTANT SEXPERT

Sexual Headache Identified

Doctors in Germany have identified the explosive pain that strikes some men just before orgasm, saying it could be related to the dilation of blood vessels. The headaches affect around 1 percent of the population, and most sufferers are men ages 20 to 25 or 35 to 45. They can be relieved with beta-blockers or painkillers, or by taking sex more slowly, doctors advise.

Eat Right, Look Good

If you plan to have great sex for the rest of your life, you want to look good doing it, right? Add a couple of servings a week of these fountain-of-youth foods.

Sunflower seeds. These salty wonders have the highest natural vitamin E content of any food around. "Vitamin E is one of the most important nutrients around for looking younger," says Barry Swanson, Ph.D., a professor of food science at Washington State University. "No antioxidant is more effective at fighting the aging effects of free radicals."

Spinach and beans. Researchers in Australia, Indonesia, and Sweden studied the diets of 400 elderly men and women, and found that those who ate the most leafy green vegetables and beans had the fewest wrinkles. The reason? Spinach and beans are full of compounds that help prevent and repair wear and tear on your skin cells as you get older.

Grape juice. Besides providing protection from heart attack and stroke, grape juice can also help keep your middle-aged skin from sagging. "Grapes are filled with antioxidant polyphenols that help to keep your skin flexible and elastic," says Swanson.

Sweet potatoes. Overexposure to the sun is one of the primary reasons men age prematurely. But sweet potatoes may help to fight sun damage. European researchers recently found that pigments from beta-carotene–rich foods—like sweet potatoes and carrots—can build up in your skin, helping to prevent damage from ultraviolet rays.

Cheese. No wonder rats always look so young. "Cheese is one of the best foods you can eat for your teeth," says Matthew Messina, D.D.S., an American Dental Association spokesman. "It's a good source of calcium, to keep your teeth strong. Plus, eating cheese can lower the levels of bacteria in your mouth and keep your teeth clean and cavity-free," he says. Dr. Messina recommends eating at least two servings of block cheese (not the processed stuff) every week.

THE FOOD: LIVER
THE BENEFIT: BOOST YOUR SPERM COUNT WHEN IT COUNTS

It doesn't sound sexy, but ounce for ounce there are few better sources of fertility-boosting vitamin A than liver. Studies show that men who get plenty of A each day have higher sperm counts and perform better sexually than men who don't. "When your body's low on A, your sperm production goes down dramatically," says Lachance. Liver is also an excellent source of zinc. Your body expels 5 milligrams of zinc—a third of your daily requirement—every time you ejaculate, so a single amorous weekend could leave your body's zinc reserves running on empty.

THE FOOD: PEACHES
THE BENEFIT: REALLY SHAKE HER TREE

Oranges get the good press as a vitamin C source, but frozen peaches are the keener choice. And that's important if you're looking to add some deductions to your 1040. "Men who don't take in enough vitamin C produce lower-quality sperm," says Althea Zanecosky, R.D., a nutritionist in Philadelphia. University of Texas researchers found that men who consumed at least 200 milligrams of vitamin C a day had higher sperm counts than men who took in less. Vitamin C also keeps your sperm from clumping, so your boys have a better chance of reaching her egg, says Marc Goldstein, M.D., director of the Cornell Center for Male Reproductive Medicine. Keep a bag of frozen peach slices—they have more C than fresh ones do—in your freezer to dump in smoothies or add to your morning cereal. A single cup of the fruit has more than twice your daily vitamin C requirement.

YOUR 40S: STAY STRONG, STAY SENSATIONAL

THE FOOD: BLUEBERRIES
THE BENEFIT: GET SOME ERECTION PROTECTION

Forget Viagra. Mother Nature's original blue potency capsule may do even more for you. "Blueberries are one of the best foods for older men with erectile problems," says Mary Ellen Camire, Ph.D., a professor of food science at the University of Maine. "They're loaded with soluble fiber, which helps push excess cholesterol through your digestive system before it can be broken down, absorbed, and deposited along the walls of your arteries," she says. "They're also packed with compounds that help relax your blood vessels, improving circulation." The benefit of lower cholesterol and better bloodflow? More blood to the penis and stronger erections as you grow older. For maximum potency and performance, Camire recommends eating a serving of blueberries (fresh or blended into a drink) at least three or four times a week.

THE FOOD: BREAKFAST CEREAL

THE BENEFIT: PUT MORE SNAP, CRACKLE, AND POP IN YOUR SEX LIFE

Too tired for sex? Check the label on your morning cereal and make sure you're eating a brand loaded with thiamin and riboflavin. Both vitamins help you use energy efficiently, so you'll stop falling asleep in the recliner while watching *Everybody Loves Raymond.* "Thiamin and riboflavin are also vital for the nervous system to function properly," says Ayoob. Better nerve function translates into more stimulation and pleasure during sex. "As you get older, your body has a harder time absorbing the vitamins that keep your nervous system operating at its peak, so you often need to increase your intake," says Lachance. Fortified breads and cereals are also high in niacin, a vitamin that's essential for the secretion of histamine—a chemical your body needs in order to trigger explosive sneezes and orgasms. God bless you.

THE FOOD: STEAK

THE BENEFIT: KEEP YOUR RELATIONSHIP SIZZLING

Sparks can dwindle after you've been with the same person for a decade or two. An easy way to reignite the relationship? Visit your favorite steak house and sup on some lean sirloin. "The protein in the meat will naturally boost levels of dopamine and norepinephrine, two chemicals in the brain that heighten sensitivity during sex," says Ward. Your steak's also stuffed with zinc—a mineral that boosts libido by reducing your body's production of a hormone called prolactin, which may interfere with arousal. And best of all, eating red meat can help boost your testosterone level while limiting your body's production of SHBG (sex hormone binding globulin)—a substance that prevents bloodflow to the penis and reduces male sexual stamina.

THE FOOD: CHOCOLATE

THE BENEFIT: AT LONG LAST, YOU'RE A SENSITIVE GUY

After your steak, finish the evening with a couple of pieces of dark chocolate. The cocoa in chocolate contains methylxanthines, stimulants that increase your body's sensitivity—ensuring that your skin registers even the slightest touch or movement against it. Chocolate also contains phenylethylamine, a chemical that can give you a slight natural high. "For many people, the feeling is similar to the sensations you experience when you first fall in love," says Ward.

The Better Sex Workout

The complete fitness program to build muscles
that turn her on—and set her off

BY LOU SCHULER

ON THE ONE HAND, SEX IS EASY. You don't have to look like a stud to service your filly. Even whales can hump. And when a lifetime of overeating and underexercising gets your dauber down, there's always that blue pill.

But that doesn't mean sex can't be made better with some out-side-the-bedroom effort. Increase your endurance and you'll turn your traditional bump-and-grind into an extended dance remix. Add muscle mass and she'll ask you to keep the lights on. And if you build some serious strength and muscle power, you'll discover that sex per-formed vertically is more versatile than the traditional geometry. "Get a room" takes on new meaning when every closet, airplane lavatory, and voting booth is a potential love shack.

The following exercises and workout ideas from trainer Don Alessi will help you become a better sexual athlete. And the novel sex positions we've found will help you prove it. That means more op-portunities for you and more pleasure for her. If she's been closing her eyes and thinking of England, your new sex-specific fitness will con-vince her to open them and speak French.

SUCK IT UP

If sex were an IQ test, you might find this question: A protruding male belly is to female sexual arousal as . . .

A. A puncture is to a balloon

B. A Chevy on blocks in the front yard is to property values

C. An unchained Doberman is to efficient postal delivery

D. All of the above (the correct answer)

One exercise that helps you hold it in is the kneeling vacuum. It strengthens the deepest abdominal muscle (the transversus abdominis), allowing you to thrust deeper during sex (because holding back the fat unsheathes more of your sword) and present a more dynamic profile before and after.

BE A HOOVER. Get on the floor on your hands and knees. Exhale and draw your belly in. Simultaneously perform a Kegel, contracting the pelvic muscles you'd use to stop the flow of urine in midstream. Hold for 10 to 60 seconds while breathing. Rest for up to a minute, then repeat. Do 10 of these contractions, or up to 5 minutes with the muscles contracted.

> **INSTANT SEXPERT**
>
> ## The Myth of Bigfoot
>
> The theory that small-footed men have smaller penises has been debunked. A study in the *British Journal of Urology* measured the penises and feet of 104 men—and found no link at all. Investigations are continuing into whether there is any link between nose, hand, and genital size. Average erect penis length: 6.4 inches.

NOW YOU'RE READY FOR: WOMAN-ON-TOP POSITIONS. Granted, you don't even need to be awake to do the most basic female-superior position (provided you sleep on your back), but with better abdominal control, you can do this more active variation: You're kneeling, she's straddling you, and the two of you are more or less face-to-face.

GET LOOSE

You don't need to be a yogi to lay pipe, but the more flexible you are, the better. Most men have tight hip flexors, the muscles on the front of the pelvis. And tightness anywhere near the pelvis cramps your style—literally. The kneeling hip-flexor stretch (shown in "The Sex Exercises" on pages 12 to 13) takes care of that problem.

(continued on page 14)

The Sex Exercises

The assignment we gave trainer Don Alessi (alessifit.com) couldn't have been more exotic: Come up with cool exercises to help turn a man into a mack daddy. He delivered a set of interesting, challenging moves, although his first suggestion is as basic as drawing breath: Improve your endurance. "Sex requires about $1\frac{1}{2}$ times the oxygen it takes to read this magazine," says Alessi. (Golf, by comparison, is three times as strenuous as sex.) Since the average guy can sling pork for about a quarter of an hour, your first step on the path to performance sex is making sure you can go longer.

Kneeling hip-flexor stretch: As your left (front) knee goes forward, you'll feel the stretch on the right side of your pelvis. Leaning back is more advanced and deepens the stretch. Hold for 15 to 30 seconds on each side.

Kneeling Hip-Flexor Stretch

Bending side press: Use two hands to hoist the barbell or EZ-curl bar to your shoulder, then balance it as you press it overhead. Do six to eight reps with your weaker arm (your left if you're right-handed), then repeat the set with your strong arm.

Bending Side Press

Wide-grip Romanian deadlift: Using a wide, overhand grip, lower the bar below your knees, bending them slightly and keeping your back flat. Thrust your hips forward as you return. Do this once or twice a week.

Dumbbell vice-grip pullover: See the instructions on the next page. If you still need more wrist work after doing both variations of this exercise, try the standard wrist curl, pausing for 2 seconds at full contraction.

Wide-Grip Romanian Deadlift

Dumbbell Vice-Grip Pullover

EZ-Curl-Bar Biceps Curl/Shoulder Press

EZ-curl-bar biceps curl/shoulder press: With a shoulder-width, underhand grip, curl to your shoulders, then press overhead. Do sets of nine, seven, five, seven, and nine reps.

NOW YOU'RE READY FOR: DOGGY-STYLE WITH A DIFFERENCE. Rear-entry sex is usually a better deal for the man than for the woman, unless she really wants to watch TV. (Something to think about next time she wants to catch *Gilmore Girls*.) But if you put your hands to use—stroking things that aren't conveniently located when you're in this position—you'll earn sensitive-guy points . . . and still get that terrific southern exposure.

SHOULDER THE LOAD

A 300-pound bench press is nice, but it won't make you better in bed. A little more strength and stability in some key muscle groups goes a long way. The bending side press strengthens your shoulders and triceps, opening you up to some interesting variations on the face-to-face theme. It also builds stability in the quadratus lumborum muscles of your lower back, which control rotation of your hips.

NOW YOU'RE READY FOR: ENTRY-LEVEL DOMINANCE. It's not something you can talk about with your buddies at the gym. ("Hey, Jack, those guns are looking huge. Tell me, does your wife ever ask you to hold her down and make her wear a blindfold?") But some women do like the sensation of being powerless. If yours is one (and she's willing

---

INSTANT SEXPERT

Toy Story

Buying a sex toy for your girl-friend is a lot like buying her any other present—you have to think about what she wants, not you (Remember how she reacted when you got her that riding lawn mower for Christmas? You're looking for the opposite reaction.) If the sex toy's meant to turn her on, then go for a vibrator designed specifically for women. Check out Candida Royalle's site at www.royalle.com, and look for the Natural Contours line. For tips on buying and using your toys, check out *The Good Vibrations Guide to Sex* (Cathy Winks and Anne Semans, Cleis Press). If you're buying a toy to watch her use on herself, think about what she can accommodate comfortably—something the width of your two fingers placed together is a good start. But whatever you do, drop a few hints first to test how she responds. She should feel this is an addition to your sex life—not something that's just for your benefit.

to put this in writing beforehand, just to be on the safe side), try holding her hands over her head during the act.

STAND AND DELIVER

Nothing separates the players from the spectators like stunt sex. You can't possibly hoist a woman off the floor and conjugate her verbs without some serious strength. Here's how much: When you have sex standing up, you're thrusting while supporting most of her weight, as well as most of yours. (If you actually left your feet with each thrust, you'd be lifting all of her plus all of you.) That's a load. You have to be really strong to pull this off, and you need to have a lot of strength endurance to keep it going long enough to earn your standing O.

The wide-grip Romanian deadlift is a classic strength-builder for guys interested in tricky wicking, because it shores up the lower back, gluteals, and hamstrings, all of which are key to performing vertically.

BULK UP TO BOINK UP. Follow the instructions (shown in "The Sex Exercises" on pages 12 to 13) for this lift, and use these sets and reps.

Advanced variation: Pull the bar up so hard that at the end of the repetition you come up on your toes and shrug your shoulders. This brings your upper trapezius and calves into the movement.

SET	REPS	LOAD
1	10	Light (could easily do 15 reps)
2	6	Moderate
3	4	Really heavy
4	6	Light (could easily do 12 reps)
5	8	Heavy (20% more than you used for set 2)

NOW YOU'RE READY FOR: THE WHEELBARROW. It's not a third-date move, but if she's adventurous (and in shape), have her rest her forearms on a slatted chair while holding on tightly to the slats. You pick her up and enter her from behind while she wraps her legs around your hips. Chiropractors love this one, so make sure your hands support her hips firmly, taking some strain off her lower back.

GIVE HER A HAND

Let's say you've achieved all the sex-centric fitness goals we've laid out so far—flat stomach, great flexibility, strong shoulders, gluteals that could crack walnuts. And let's say you're putting them all to use with a coworker in the office-supply closet.

She's close to climax, but your grip is giving out. Which explains why she hits the floor 2 seconds later, and instead of having an orgasm she'll never forget, she'll be picking Post-its out of her private parts for the next week. All because you have less-than-ideal hand strength and endurance.

Save her that awkward moment by finishing your workouts with the dumbbell vice-grip pullover (shown in "The Sex Exercises" on pages 12 to 13), which strengthens your forearms, hands, and fingers by forcing you to do a familiar exercise in an unusual way.

HOLD IT RIGHT THERE. Grab a pair of light dumbbells (about 30 percent lighter than you'd use for normal pullovers) and hold them like this: Wrap three fingers around the shaft of the dumbbell, just beneath the weight plates at one end, with your thumb and forefinger around the plates themselves. Now lie on your back on a bench, holding the dumbbells over your forehead, palms facing backward and elbows bent 90 degrees. Slowly lower the dumbbells behind your head until your upper arms are nearly parallel to the floor. Pause for 2 full seconds, then pull the dumbbells back to the starting position. Your elbows stay at a 90-degree angle throughout the movement.

Do a set of eight to 12 repetitions, then switch to this grip: Hold the dumbbells with your thumb and forefinger on the shaft and the other three fingers on the dumbbell plates. Your palms face each other in this variation. Do another set of eight to 12 repetitions, and repeat both sets if you want. Try this exercise once or twice a week.

NOW YOU'RE READY FOR: FREE-STANDING SEX. It's difficult to enter from this position, so a good strategy is to start by kneeling on the floor. She straddles you, Tab A finds Slot B, and then you stand up, with your hands beneath her thighs or buttocks for support and her legs around your hips. Find a wall to lean against, or to lean her against; otherwise, this quickie will be your most strenuous workout of the week.

ARM YOURSELF

Nature meant for sex to be a multisensory experience. We quickly learn that saying the wrong things ("If we hurry, we can catch *Sports-Center!*"), wearing the wrong fragrance ("It was on sale at Sam's Club!"), or touching her in the wrong places ("What the hell's a Post-it doing down here?") sucks the carnality right out of the air.

Your visual presentation, though, has little to do with what you're doing in the heat of the moment and everything to do with how you prepare for it. That's where the EZ-curl-bar biceps curl/shoulder press (shown in "The Sex Exercises" on pages 12 to 13) comes in. Our exclusive survey *(continued on page 20)*

INSTANT SEXPERT

Moisture Management

Nothing brings out the excited—dare we say, giddy—inner child in a guy like a woman who excites easily. But what if that woman is your wife and one day her pipes go dry? There's no need to throw a tantrum or sulk. Try lubricants—an underrated element of sexual pleasure. Your partner may not be as excited any more, you may not be giving her enough time to feel turned on, or there may be a health problem, in which case she should speak to her doctor, especially if she's experiencing pain during sex too.

By drawing attention to her lack of lubrication, you may be putting her under pressure, causing her to "dry up." Make her feel great about herself all the time (not just when you want sex), and talk with her about what tends to make her feel sexier. There are also external factors that can lead to dryness: if your wife's going through menopause, has changed contraceptive methods, is pregnant, or has given birth recently. Whatever the cause, she needs your support.

3 Million Women Can't Be Wrong

When guys want to impress guys, they try to build arms so big that even Hans Blix couldn't miss them. But when guys want to impress women . . . well, there isn't such a clear game plan. So we asked readers of *Cosmopolitan* magazine to help us formulate one.

Here's how they responded to this question: "Which muscles on a man absolutely make you melt?"

BODY PART	PERCENTAGE OF RESPONSES
Abs	32.47
Biceps	17.53
Shoulders	16.88
Butt	9.09
Back	7.79
Chest	6.49
Triceps	4.55
Calves	2.60
Thighs	2.60
Neck	0.00

Okay, so even the Democratic Party's pollsters could've predicted that abs would win. What was interesting was the many ways that women described the parts of the abs they like to see well-developed in a man:

• "The muscle that runs diagonally from hip to crotch."

• "The muscle that sticks out near the hips—yummy!"

• "Lower abs, near his package."

• "The muscle lines below the belly button."

In other words, if you've been crunching like a bowl of Grape-Nuts to build a babe-worthy six-pack, it's time to lower your sights. Try this two-exercise routine, along with the kneeling vacuum described previously, to work your obliques and lower abs. Do it twice a week and see if www.yourbadself.org attracts a few more leers.

Lateral trunk raise: builds the muscles on the sides of your waist
Position yourself perpendicular to an exercise bench so your left forearm
rests on the bench and the outer side of your left leg is near the floor.
Rest your right leg on your left leg, and put your right hand on your
head. Now lift your left hip so your body forms a straight line from your
left shoulder through your left ankle. Pause, then lower yourself. Do one
to three sets of 10 to 12 repetitions on each side.

Lateral trunk raise

Drawbridge: builds the muscles surrounding your pelvis
Lie on your back with your legs straight up in the air, feet together,
knees locked. (Novice exercisers should do this one without shoes.)
Contract your abs so your lower back is flat on the floor. Now slowly
lower your legs as far as you can before you feel your lower back rise up
off the floor. Stop and lift your legs over your hips again. Once you have
a feel for it, do three sets of as many repetitions as you can, taking a full
8 seconds to lower your legs to the stopping point.

Sex and Death

Sex isn't particularly dangerous to your cardiovascular system—at least not in Wales, where researchers estimate that sex will kill about one man in 580, assuming all of them have sex once a week for 50 years. Those getting less action are more likely to die of a heart attack during sex (although they have the lowest overall risk of stroke, for reasons unknown).

About 1 percent of all heart attacks occur during sex, according to research by Graham Jackson, M.D., of St. Thomas's Hospital in London, and roughly 75 percent of deaths during sex involve a new partner, usually in an extramarital affair. That means, of course, that 25 percent of coital corpses earned a toe tag from sex with the old lady. We guess that beats a having coronary while cleaning the gutters.

An orgasm, according to researchers, requires exertion equivalent to climbing a set of stairs. Talk about your stairway to heaven. . . .

of *Cosmopolitan* magazine's sexually voracious readers shows that women like to see buff biceps and shoulders. Here's how to give the audience what it wants.

BUILD THE BETTER LOVE HANDLES. Grab an EZ-curl bar with an underhand grip and hold it in front of your thighs, your elbows very slightly bent. Curl the bar as high as you can while keeping your elbows against your sides. Now pull your elbows forward so the bar rises to shoulder level, then press it overhead, so at the end your arms are straight and the bar is directly over your ears. You should be able to draw a straight line from the bar through your ears, hips, and ankles.

NOW YOU'RE READY FOR: CHAIR SEX. You're on the edge of the chair, she's straddling you, her hands all over your shoulders and biceps. It's not a technically difficult position, which is why your muscles make it either memorable or forgettable. (Although it wouldn't hurt to trim those nose hairs.)

Cock Sure

How to live to 90 and die having sex

BY HUGH O'NEILL

NONE OF THE FOLLOWING INFORMATION about erection excellence is of the slightest personal interest to me. Even though I'm on the back nine of life, I'm blessed with function every bit as effervescent as I had when I was at JFK High. Really. I swear. It's true. Really. But apparently, studies show that lots of men my age just aren't stallions like me. And apparently, some men are ashamed to admit it.

"By age 40, about 40 percent of men have some erectile dysfunction, and the number goes up about 10 percent with each advancing decade," says Richard Spark, M.D., an associate clinical professor of medicine at Harvard medical school and author of *Sexual Health for Men*. Of course, the degree of the problem varies greatly. For most, Ol' Reliable still shows up, but he's not as quick to the ready position and is a bit less still than when he wowed Annette from Theta Delta.

"Virtually all men see some age-associated decline," says Culley Carson, M.D., a professor of urology at the University of North Carolina at Chapel Hill. "But if you lead a healthy life, you can stay sexually vigorous for a long time." So, purely in the interest of public service, I asked experts how the warranty on Wonderboy could be extended.

What's that? Why worry, there's always Viagra? Well, no. It's a great drug, but it's not for everybody. Some men can't take it because it's dangerous in combination with heart medications. It also has side effects, works only in some cases, and costs about $10 a pop, so to speak. Further, Daddy's little helper takes about an hour to kick in— by which time the plane often has landed. But there's an even more compelling reason to go natural: If you live an erection-friendly life, you'll fortify most every other body part.

FOUR NEW ERECTION PROTECTORS

Urologists believe that the well-tested principles that protect blood vessels also give erections their best shot at remaining bodacious. Further, because the gradual erosions of aging seem to play a role in erection strength, slowing the processes that make us old should also keep us hard. You already know the importance of exercise, weight control, and cholesterol management in staying healthy, so we won't lecture you again about them. Instead, here are four new strategies:

1. CONTROL BLOOD PRESSURE. Erectile dysfunction (ED) is both more common and more severe in men with high blood pressure. According to a study published in the *Journal of Urology*, chronic hypertension is the biggest threat to Iron John because it puts vessels under constant stress. "Over the years, higher pressure steals elasticity from the vessel walls, including the ones in your penis," says Ridwan Shabsigh, M.D., an associate professor of urology at Columbia University. "This makes them less able to dilate and fill with blood."

Working out and maintaining a healthy weight are the most obvious ways to moderate blood pressure. But certain foods also affect it. Avoid simple carbohydrates, such as cakes, refined pasta, and white breads. These burn quickly, which spikes blood sugar, which creates a surge of insulin, which raises blood pressure. Instead, eat complex carbohydrates, including . . .

> • **Colorful fruits and vegetables:** Strawberries, blueberries, tomatoes, dark green leafy vegetables, oranges, grapes, apricots, yams, and watermelons. All of these burn slowly and evenly.

Erections at Every Age

AGE	ANGLE (ABOVE OR BELOW HORIZONTAL)
30	10°
40	0°
50	−15°
60	−20°
70	−30°

• **Oatmeal:** There are compelling studies linking oatmeal and oat bran to lower blood pressure.

• **Bananas:** Top it with a banana, and you're set for the day. Bananas are good sources of potassium, a shortage of which has been linked to high blood pressure.

The other big factor influencing blood pressure is stress. "When you're chronically anxious, stress hormones such as epinephrine and adrenaline narrow your blood vessels and raise the pressure inside them," says Dr. Carson. "And anything that does this works against your erection."

2. MAKE MORE NITRIC OXIDE. This is a signaling substance that starts the process of blood-vessel dilation. "It increases bloodflow, prevents fatty deposits from sticking to arteries, and reduces constriction," says John P. Cooke, M.D., an associate professor of medicine at Stanford University medical school. "An inability to produce it has been linked to impotence." Low levels of nitric oxide are seen in diabetics, smokers, and men with low levels of testosterone. There are a number of things you can do to ensure an adequate supply:

• **Eat foods rich in L-arginine.** This is the amino acid necessary to form nitric oxide. While there's no conclusive evidence, it can't hurt to eat foods that contain L-arginine, such as beans, fish, soy, egg whites, chicken, lean red meat, and peanuts.

• **Swallow more omega-3s.** These fatty acids improve blood pressure. Salmon and olive oil are good sources, as are walnuts.

• **Build muscle.** For older men, Dr. Cooke recommends isotonic exercise. Jogging, walking, and swimming rather than pushups, pullups, and bench presses are part of a pro-erection plan.

3. DEFEND AGAINST FREE RADICALS. These are damaging molecules that your cells produce in the normal course of burning oxygen. They undermine the resiliency of blood vessels and, with it, your potency. To keep them from running amok:

• **Trim the steak.** The saturated fat in beef burns fast, oxidizes quickly, and produces more free radicals than our systems can handle.

• **Eat more antioxidants.** Nutrients lycopene, beta-carotene, vitamin C, and vitamin E are the scourge of free radicals. Carrots, tomatoes, spinach, grapes, and zucchini are especially full of them, as is soy.

4. STEM THE DECLINE OF SEX HORMONES. In our middle years, levels of two key cell-spackling hormones—human growth hormone (HGH) and DHEA, a precursor to testosterone—decline. So does testosterone. Their waning leaves our cells more vulnerable to assault from free radicals and less able to repair themselves. To boost testosterone naturally, adopt these habits and maintain them for life:

• **Get more sleep.** Since most of our HGH is secreted while we sleep, snoozing may help you stay young and sexually sterling. Aspire to get 8 hours a night.

• **Have more sex.** In one of life's great feedback loops, testosterone makes us want sex, and sex raises our levels of testosterone. So the more erections you have, the more erections you'll have. Plus, every time fresh oxygen-rich blood enters the penis, it flushes away harmful collagens that cause scar tissue, says Dr. Shabsigh.

• **Lift more weight.** Generally, the more muscle mass you have, the higher your level of testosterone.

SEVEN ANTISOFTENING SOLUTIONS

If you're already experiencing erection problems, don't panic. For the majority of men, there are effective therapies. But first you have to ask for help. Unfortunately, only one in four men does.

"Erection difficulties can be a harbinger of serious medical problems, including heart disease, diabetes, prostate trouble, or depression," says Dr. Carson. If diagnosed early, they're often manageable. But the longer they go undetected, the worse they can become.

The same idea applies to emotional issues. "Sometimes your penis is trying to tell you that something is wrong with your relationship," says Alon Gratch, Ph.D., a Manhattan psychologist.

For these reasons, don't let your doctor just toss you some Viagra samples and send you on your way. Instead, press him to pinpoint what's causing your ED. Many men benefit from couple's therapy. Communication and the support that inevitably ensues can

INSTANT SEXPERT

Fast and Furious

If you're looking for someone to blame for your premature ejaculation, you might consider your right hand, man. Many guys learn to masturbate in secret, and as a consequence learn to come quickly. That's a hard habit to break. Being anxious about it doesn't help either.

To prolong your endurance, stop masturbating just before you are about to come, and vary the speed and pressure with which you touch yourself. Make sure you're relaxed and able to wank somewhere you won't get stressed or concerned about interruptions. Remember, it's not a timed exercise; it's about enjoying yourself.

be a remarkable antidote. If noninvasive approaches fail, consider these alternatives:

1. VIAGRA. It has worked for 10 million American men. But if it doesn't immediately work for you, don't give up. According to a study performed at the University of Maryland Medical Center, almost 40 percent of men who didn't initially respond to Viagra had better success after receiving more careful instructions or increasing the standard 50-milligram dose. Among the most common mistakes is taking it after a large or high-fat meal, which can interfere with the body's absorption of the drug.

2. "SUPER VIAGRAS." By the time you read this, the FDA may already have approved two new drugs, vardenafil and tadalafil. Vardenafil works more quickly (generally in less than an hour) and is not affected by food in the stomach. Tadalafil lasts longer, up to 36 hours. (For more hard facts on tadalafil and vardenafil, turn to page 28.)

3. VACUUM DEVICES. Before the advent of Viagra, vacuum devices were the leading treatment for ED. They consist of an airtight plastic cylinder with an attached pump. You slide your penis into the tube and use the pump to suck all the air out of the cylinder. Since nature hates a vacuum, the negative pressure in the tube draws blood into the penis, causing an erection. Granted, this precludes a fast-and-furious quickie on the picnic table at the Davy Crockett Overlook, but it works well.

4. INJECTION THERAPY. Yes, the injection goes into the penis. But it's not as bad as it sounds. "Most of my patients are pleasantly surprised," says Dr. Shabsigh. You shoot up before sex with a medication called Caverject. Generally, the shot works in 20 minutes, and you stay hard for up to an hour. Men with nerve-related impotence respond best.

5. INTRAURETHRAL THERAPY. The same medication is delivered another way. A small, soft pellet is inserted into the tip of the penis and urged onward by gentle rolling. It makes the vessels dilate and welcome blood. In general, according to Dr. Shabsigh, this is not as effective as an injection.

6. HORMONE THERAPY. Though testosterone therapy is controversial, for erection problems caused by low levels of this important male hormone, supplementation can help. The latest method of delivery is AndroGel, a testosterone gel that's rubbed on the shoulders.

7. PENILE IMPLANTS. There are two types. For one, bendable, semi-rigid rods are surgically installed into the penis. When you're ready for romance, you simply snap the rocket into launch position. The other type involves putting inflatable tubes into the penis, a pump in the scrotum, and a fluid reservoir in the lower part of the stomach. To charm your sweetheart, you just squeeze your scrotum a few times, causing fluid from the reservoir to enter the tubes.

With any luck, you'll never have to weigh these options, especially if you keep in mind that durable vigor is earned through countless small attentions paid over years. Singly, each of the erection protectors outlined here may seem modest, but in concert and over time, they'll accrue like wealth.

Sex Drugs: Rock 'n' Roll!

Faster-acting, longer-lasting, more potent—brace yourself
for the "Super Viagras"

BY JOE KITA

AFTER SURGEONS REMOVED 53-year-old Bob Rozman's
cancerous prostate gland, he couldn't get an erection. He tried Viagra.
He tried penile injections. And he tried penis pumps. But he and his
wife still went 2½ years without having sex. Rozman thought it was
hopeless until he became involved in a clinical trial of a new erection
drug called Cialis.

"I took one pill," he recounts. "Then my wife and I had dinner,
we talked, and later on that evening we had sex. It was all very natural
and spontaneous. It was unbelievable."

Two new erection-enhancing drugs are expected to receive FDA
approval some time in late 2003 or early 2004. One is tadalafil (brand
name Cialis) from Lilly Icos, and the other is vardenafil (brand name
undecided) from Bayer and GlaxoSmithKline. Both are taken orally
and contain the same chemical agent as Viagra, but each has been
molecularly tweaked to work differently, if not better. This is good
news, because despite the fanfare and interest Viagra has generated,
90 percent of men with erectile dysfunction (ED) are reportedly still
untreated. Either they're too uncomfortable discussing the problem
with their doctors, or they've tried Viagra and it had little effect.
These new drugs will not only expand awareness through increased
advertising and publicity, but also broaden the choices available for
doctors and patients.

"We'll be able to experiment a little and see which one a man best responds to," says Gregory Broderick, M.D., a professor of urology at the Mayo Clinic in Jacksonville, Florida.

Below you'll find our analysis of the most important properties of each new drug. Keep in mind that there are still no completed trials pitting them against Viagra. Even given FDA approval and further study, American men will be the true lab rats.

WAITING FOR WOOD

It typically takes Viagra about 1 hour to take effect, which means if Hilde suddenly gets horny, you'll either have to stall or engage in some lengthy foreplay. Vardenafil appears to be faster acting, with peak effects usually between 30 and 45 minutes. Cialis is a bit slower than

Beyond Viagra

Although vardenafil and Cialis are exciting developments, they still act in the same old way: by facilitating bloodflow to the penis. The next evolution in sex drugs will be dramatically different, because they'll act centrally—on the wiring in the brain instead of the plumbing in the genitals. The first one of these drugs we'll most likely see (within 2 years) is Uprima, which has been developed by Abbott Laboratories and is already available in Europe. Its active ingredient is apomorphine, but it's not related to any opiate or narcotic. Originally used to treat Parkinson's disease, it somehow tinkers with the brain's centers for arousal and pleasure.

"You put a small amount under your tongue," explains Wayne Hellstrom, M.D., "and it works very quickly [in 12 to 15 minutes]. There can be some side effects, though, such as nausea and vomiting. Overall, I don't think it's as effective as Viagra-type drugs, but it represents a new method of treatment. Ten years from now, I see doctors using a combination of therapies to treat erectile dysfunction."

vardenafil and Viagra, according to Wayne Hellstrom, M.D., a professor of urology at Tulane University medical center.

A complicating factor can be the amount of food in your stomach. If it's full, oral medications may take longer to work. Viagra is like this. For best results, doctors advise taking it 3 hours after eating. Vardenafil appears to have the same limitation, but Cialis seems unaffected by food. "Even after a heavy, fatty meal, its absorption rate and onset of action are the same as with an empty stomach," says J. Francois Eid, M.D., a clinical associate professor at Weill Cornell medical college. "This is a particular advantage for diabetics, who have a slower rate of gastric emptying." And given the connection between diabetes and impotence, that can be a saving factor.

None of these drugs causes instant, mindless erections. The results are facilitated but not assured. Stimulation is still required. But one of the most common complaints about Viagra is that sex must occur within about 4 hours after taking it. For men with ED, this extra pressure can add to performance anxiety and even thwart intercourse. But both of the new drugs appear to be longer lasting. Vardenafil has a window of about 5 hours, and Cialis may hang around in the body for up to 36 hours.

In fact, in Europe Cialis is known as the "weekend pill." Take it Friday night and you're ready for action through Sunday. The promise of such spontaneity is a great advantage.

"Patients who've taken both describe one as a quick fix and the other as making them feel normal again," says Dr. Eid.

JACK'S A DULL BOY

Hours of his life the average guy will spend . . .

Working: Having sex:

88,725   1,662

Quick Comparison

You know what erection-enhancement drugs do *for* you. Here's what they do *to* you.

	VIAGRA	VARDENAFIL	CIALIS
Onset of action	About 60 min	30–45 min	45–75 min
Eating beforehand	3 hrs	3 hrs	Anytime
Duration	4 hrs	5 hrs	Up to 36 hrs
Nasal congestion	Yes	Yes	Yes
Facial flushing	Yes	Yes	Yes
Stomach upset	Yes	Yes	Yes
Headache	Yes	Yes	Yes
Hazy vision	Yes	No	No
Back pain	No	No	Yes
General achiness	No	No	Yes
Heart risk for men taking nitrates	Yes	Yes	Yes

AND THE LUCKY LUMBERJACKS ARE . . .

Viagra is a wonderful drug for men who, shall we say, are just a little impotent. According to Dr. Broderick, it's up to 83 percent effective for men with one or two risk factors for ED (e.g., high blood pressure, being over 50 years of age). But when a man has additional complications, such as hypertension or diabetes, the effectiveness of Viagra declines to 50 percent or less. "We're hoping these new drugs will enable us to treat patients with multiple risk factors better than Viagra," he says.

These drugs could be for sale in drugstores as quickly as 3 weeks

after being blessed by the FDA. The price will probably be compa-
rable to Viagra's. Pamela Weir, director of external communications
for Bayer, says her company has a "very aggressive" plan in place for
promoting its drug once it's approved, as does Lilly Icos.

"Overall, I look at all this very positively," says Dr. Hellstrom.
"Despite Viagra's great success, only one in 10 men with erectile dysfunction has talked to his doctor about it. Out of that group, only half
are taking medication. There's still a huge untapped zone of guys who
are sitting on the fence."

No doubt these new drugs will finally help more of them get off.

Members Only

A Conversation with Michael Castleman

Show us a guy who is happy with his penis size, and we'll show you a man in the minority. The longing for a larger member is so innate that few guys can pinpoint the age at which they first began wanting more long in their dong.

But is a longer, thicker penis really necessary for pleasing women? Is it counterproductive for guys to worry about size? And if so, what should they be worrying about instead? We asked Michael Castleman, former editor of the *Playboy* magazine Advisor and author of the book *Great Sex* (Rodale, 2004), about man's phallic fantasy.

Compared with times past, do you think men's feelings about penis size has stayed the same, shrunk, or grown?
Men definitely care more about size than they used to. If you look at Renaissance sculpture of male nudes—for example, Michelangelo's *David*—the statues are all pretty modestly endowed. In fact, the *David* is downright small. Men comparing themselves to the *David* or other classical depictions of male nudes would think, "I'm like that or even larger, so I'm fine."

Today—except for comparatively fleeting glimpses of other guys in locker rooms—other than their own, the only penises heterosexual men get to see up close and personal, flaccid and erect, for extended periods of time are the penises in pornography. The men in porn are cast not for their acting talent but for their size. They're all Goliaths, so all the Davids of the world think, "My God, I'm a peanut."

I've interviewed many urologists about penis size. They see more penises than anyone. They all agree that about 5 percent of men are extra large, 90 percent of men are average, and 5 percent are small. But in surveys, the vast majority of men say they're too small.

Why do you think men are so self-conscious about penis size?
I blame porn for inundating men with images of super-huge penises that very few guys can measure up to. I've answered sex questions for over 20 years now, starting out as a sex counselor, then for 5 years as a contributor to *Playboy*'s Advisor column, and recently, for several Web sites. Among men who ask questions, one of the most common has always been "My penis is too small. How can I make it larger?" Over the past few years, I've seen more of these questions, in part because the Internet makes it easier to ask sex questions, but in part, I believe, because men have such easy access to pornographic images on the Internet—and the penises they see are all much larger than theirs, which convinces them that they're too small.

Have there been definitive studies that debunk the size myth?
There have been many medical studies of penis size. Here's the consensus: Measuring along the top of the penis, from the base of the shaft to the tip—and not pulling on the penis to stretch it or pushing the ruler into the gut—the typical adult flaccid penis measures $2^{1}/_{2}$ to 4 inches in length, with a similar circumference. The typical erection measures 5 to $6^{1}/_{2}$ inches, with a circumference of 3 to $4^{1}/_{2}$ inches. Flaccid size has nothing to do with erection size. It's quite possible to have a flaccid penis on the small side and a $6^{1}/_{2}$-inch erection. In general, the smaller the flaccid penis, the more length and girth it gains in erection.

And yet, none of us believe that.

Yeah, the studies are there, but men don't believe them—even me. I may be a longtime professional sex educator married to a woman who thinks my average-size penis is just fine. But I'm still a pretty regular guy. When I look in the mirror, I can't help thinking, "I wish I were better hung. I mean, an extra inch couldn't hurt."

Men care a great deal about size, but as far as women's sexual satisfaction is concerned, the vast majority of women get the most erotic enjoyment from direct clitoral stimulation—not intercourse. Now most women enjoy intercourse, but they are most likely to express orgasm through direct clitoral stimulation. In fact, survey after survey shows that fewer than half of perfectly normal women have orgasms from intercourse, no matter how long it lasts and no matter how large the man's penis.

Some guys I know have started worrying about girth. Is girth more important to women than length?

Women feel the same about length and girth: They wish men would stop obsessing about penis size. Women are more likely to complain that guys are too big than too small. Over the years, I've interviewed and answered questions from men with porn-size penises. Every one of them has said the same thing: They consider their phone-pole endowments a burden. Women take one look at their erections and say, "No way you're putting that thing in me."

What are some psychological reasons why men care so much about size?

Most men have a great deal of ego and self-esteem tied up in being good lovers. Meanwhile, the surveys show that about one-third of women don't have much interest in sex or find it difficult to become aroused, and that about one-quarter have difficulty with orgasm. So many men get feedback from women that something is sexually wrong, that sex isn't as easy, fun, and orgasmic as the media make it seem—and not just porn, but all media: movies, TV, popular music, books—everything. Men take a great deal of responsibility for the quality of sex. When the women in their lives let them know that something is wrong, most men infer that something is wrong with *them*—and many figure it must be their size. They're convinced they must be too small.

What should men be focusing on instead of size?

The keys to great sex include: (1) personal cleanliness, (2) leisurely, playful, whole-body, massage-oriented sensuality, (3) during intercourse, a slow, sensual rhythm, and (4) less focus on your penis and more on your tongue.

You wouldn't believe the number of women who complain that the guy smells bad, needs a shower, or has bad breath. Cleanliness may not be next to godliness, but it's an important part of sexiness. Take a shower before sex.

Better yet, take a shower with your lover. Having a naked woman in the shower is a great visual turn-on for men. And showering is a whole-body sensual experience, so it's a turn-on for women.

As for sensuality, sure, her breasts and genitals are important. But so is the rest of her—every square inch. Most women simply cannot get really aroused and express orgasm without whole-body sensuality. Compared with men, the vast majority of women need more warm-up time before they feel interested in or comfortable with genital play. Men need to slow down, then slow down even more. I advise men to devote at least 30 minutes to kissing, hugging, rolling around, and whole-body, massage-style caresses before reaching between a woman's legs or pushing their penises into the vagina.

In porn, during intercourse, the men pump in and out furiously. That's more likely to hurt the woman than feel erotic to her. Great sex is a dance—a slow dance. Ease into her slowly. Make sure she's really wet before you attempt to enter her. If she isn't, use a commercial lubricant on both her vagina and your penis. Once you're inside her, move in a slow, sensual rhythm. Sense how she's moving. Move with her.

You mentioned tongues, too. You mean oral sex?
Your fingers and tongue are more important than your penis. Massage her all over with your hands, and instead of focusing on penis-vagina intercourse, focus on cunnilingus. Give her the gift of gentle oral sex. Most women are much more likely to be orgasmic from oral sex than from intercourse.

Going back to penises for a second: Is it true that the same man's penis, fully engorged, can differ in length from erection to erection? And is there anything a guy can do to maximize his erection?
Whether flaccid or erect, penis size depends on the amount of blood contained in the organ's central spongy tissues. The more blood, the larger you are. Many factors affect penile blood supply. A low-fat diet can increase penis size. Refraining from smoking increases your size, or should I say, smoking shrinks your penis. Being relaxed helps blood reach your penis easier because the arteries that carry blood into the penis are surrounded by smooth muscle tissue. When men feel anxious, this muscle tissue contracts, limiting bloodflow.

Let's imagine a man who has a thin, 3-inch erection and has never made a woman come during vaginal intercourse. It's his hope that, someday, without the help of vibrators, fingers, or other extraneous digits, he will bring a woman to orgasm with his penis. Is there any hope for this man?
Yes. As I mentioned, most women need direct clitoral stimulation to have orgasms—and for more than half of women, intercourse just doesn't provide it, no matter how long the act lasts or how large the man's penis. For couples who want to bring the woman to orgasm during intercourse, most sex therapists recommend intercourse in the

woman-on-top or rear-entry (doggy) position with the man or woman providing direct clitoral stimulation using a hand or vibrator.

But if you don't want anything "extraneous," here's another option. It's a variation on the man-on-top (missionary) position called the coital alignment technique (CAT). The CAT is simple: Instead of you lying on top of her chest-to-chest with your penis moving in and out more or less horizontally, you shift your body upward and to one side so that your chest is closer to one of her shoulders. With this minor change, your penis moves more up-and-down, and—here's the key to the CAT—your pubic bone, that hard thing you can feel if you press on the base of your penis, presses against her clitoris and may provide enough stimulation for her to express orgasm.

I should add that the CAT won't guarantee orgasm during intercourse. Many women simply can't reach orgasm during intercourse, period. But the CAT improves some women's ability, no matter what the man's penis size.

Any suggestions on how women can convince their men that their penis size is just fine?
I think the best thing women can do on the penis-size issue is to tell their men over and over again, "I like your penis just like it is. I like the way you look flaccid. I like the way you look erect. And I like the way your penis feels inside me."

Will men ever stop agonizing over the length of their penises?
I certainly hope so. But it's so much easier to get sexually miseducated by porn—and by friends who get their misinformation from porn—than it is to find scientifically accurate sex information. The Internet has been a great boon to good sex information, but unfortunately, that information has been buried under an avalanche of Internet porn that teaches sex all wrong. As a sex educator, I don't worry about being put out of business anytime soon.

QUICKIES

BUGS IS BIGGER; LADY BUNNIES REJOICE

Harvard researchers may have found the most viable penis-enlargement technique yet. To perform the experimental procedure, doctors remove cells from a patient's penis and replicate them in a lab. The resulting synthetic tissue is then mixed with collagen, molded to the proper shape, and surgically inserted into the penis—making it either longer or wider. Although the technique hasn't been tried in humans, researchers found that rabbits who underwent the procedure and were then placed in pens with female rabbits were able to mate 4 weeks after their surgery was completed.

MOOD-ELEVATING SEX

Semen is a natural Prozac. Consider this news from the State University of New York at Albany: A study of 293 women found that those who had sex without condoms scored better on a standard depression questionnaire than those who often used condoms. Women exposed to semen were clearly less depressed, says the lead researcher, Gordon Gallup, Ph.D. It may be because mood-altering hormones in semen are absorbed through the vagina; some have even been detected in women's blood within hours of their having sex. Gallup says he's not advocating unprotected sex as a mood lifter—sex any way you can get it triggers feel-good endorphins, after all—and besides, an STD or unwanted pregnancy is a real downer.

THE SEASON FOR SEX

Is there a chill outside? Warm up in the bedroom. According to an international study of more than a million people, children conceived

INSTANT SEXPERT

For Your Own Protection (or Lack Thereof)

Any guy who's ever heard the words "I missed my period" knows the feeling—those days spent milling around, wondering if you've just hopped the train to Unready Da-Da Land. It's an illness that can be cured only by the sight of your partner emerging from the bathroom with a smile and a just-opened tampon wrapper.

Brace yourself for some bad news: She could still be pregnant. It's unlikely, but period-like bleeding can occur during pregnancy. To reassure you both, she should take a pregnancy test—either an over-the-counter one from a drugstore or an in-office test from her doctor. Next, discuss reliable contraception options with your doctor or nurse, or at a family planning clinic.

And for anyone who's had unprotected sex, it's possible for women to purchase the morning-after pill with a simple doctor's prescription. It should never be used as a regular method of contraception, as this can damage a woman's health, but it's an option in the case of contraception failure or "accidental" unprotected sex.

in the winter live longer than children conceived during other seasons. They're also less likely to suffer from chronic illnesses.

ORGASMS: WHAT THE DOCTOR ORDERED

The optimal number of orgasms a man should have every week to stay healthy and, um, strong: 2 to 3 (at least).

Many urologists recommend that men ejaculate a minimum of two or three times a week for optimal health. "More frequent ejaculation is certainly not going to hurt," says Mark Goldstein, M.D., director of the center for male reproductive medicine at Cornell Medical Center. "Prolonged periods of abstinence can lead to chronic congestion and congestive prostatitis." Also, the magic three (or more) a week correlated to a 50 percent cut in the chances of having a stroke or heart attack. Have your doctor write a prescription. It might work.

MUSCLE UP FOR LOVE

By working one small muscle at the gym, your desk, or while

fishing, you can increase your orgasmic power and lower the risk of impotence—without getting arrested. So tone up with these techniques:

Kegel exercises are used to tone up and strengthen the pubococcygeus (PC) muscle, which is involved in orgasm and ejaculation. By performing Kegels, you can experience a stronger erection, more intense climaxes, increased power of ejaculation and help cure impotence.

You won't find a piece of equipment at the gym to build up this muscle, but luckily it doesn't need one. Schedule these into your workouts:

Find the PC Muscle

Stop and restart your urination five times in the men's room. (Those eight glasses of water a day will give you plenty of ammunition.) The muscle you're flexing is the PC, as opposed to your anal sphincter muscles.

The PC muscle runs from the pubic bone in the front to the coccyx (tail bone) in the back and lies about 2 centimeters beneath the surface, supporting the pelvic organs like a hammock. This muscle also lifts and lowers the erect penis (the same one that wags your dog's tail—the canine's PC muscle, that is).

Exercise It: The Basic Kegel Exercise

Now you've identified the muscle, skip the bathroom exercises and start doing your Kegels, which can be done anywhere and any time, as long as you're stationary.

1. Contract the pubococcygeus muscle and hold for a count of 10.

2. Now relax the muscle.

3. Repeat. Aim for at least 10 sets, several times a day. Some therapists recommend you do 100 to 300 contractions a day, but remember to start out gradually.

Here's a variation on the basic exercise.

1. Contract the PC muscle over a count of five, from relaxed to as tight as possible.

2. Relax the PC muscle for one count.

With your PC muscle firmly toned over a number of weeks, your member will be more powerful than a medieval battering ram. If you purposely contract the PC muscle during sex, it acts like the brakes on a car and can bring your ejaculation to a halt, while still allowing you to experience orgasm.

INCREASING THE QUANTITY OF YOUR EJACULATION

The intensity of the male orgasm is directly related to how much fluid you ejaculate. While the idea of going for a week without sex or masturbation may strike terror into the hearts of some men, the build-up of semen in the kegs through abstinence will guarantee a powerful ejaculation the next time you get busy in the boudoir.

If you figure that going even a day without masturbation is pretty unrealistic, you can increase the quantity of semen by prolonging the level of foreplay you engage in. During times of strong arousal, the prostate and seminal vessels produce additional semen.

While you're at work, a few sexy e-mails, pictures, or phone calls from your better half can wind you up both physically and mentally, causing your body to produce extra fluid in anticipation of that big night at home with your PC-toned pecker.

SEXY MOVER

This Pilates sequence will transform your nights of nookie. It'll strengthen your pelvic floor muscles, giving you stronger orgasms, and it serves as a warm-up exercise for other sport.

1. Go Down

"Lie on your back with your feet flat on the floor and knees bent at 90 degrees," says Lynne Robinson, Pilates instructor for England's cricket team. (No, we didn't realize they had one either.)

2. Knees Up

Put your arms by your sides and lift your knees up towards your chest, with your knees bent at 90 degrees. "Imagine yourself peeing at the same time as you pull your lower abs down towards your spine," advises Robinson.

3. Curl It

Breathe in, then breathe out while tucking your chin in, and curl your upper body off the floor. "Lift your arms so they're parallel to the ground and really stretch them forward, palms down, keeping your upper body 'open'," says Robinson.

4. Pump

Keep your shoulder-blades down on the ground, and pump arms up and down in tandem as if slapping water. Your hands should be moving about 15cm from top to bottom. Breathe in, then out, to a count of five pumps each. Do 100 reps.

For more Pilates moves, track down a copy of *The Official Control Pilates Manual* (Lynne Robinson, et al.; Macmillan).

ASK THE GIRL NEXT DOOR

Hooded Menace

Do uncircumcised penises turn women off? —BRYANT, VERMONT

Something like 65 percent of American men have been snipped as babes, so foreskins aren't something most women here think about until we happen to find one in a guy's pants. One friend whose ex-boyfriend's penis had a hood confessed to me that she didn't even notice he wasn't circumcised until she had already been sleeping with him for 2 months. When she finally noticed, she said it was "interesting and kind of exotic." Another friend who has never laid eyes or hands on a lance with a lid said she would be fascinated yet intimidated. "He'd have to show me what it does," were her exact words. So, I think that most American women are very curious and a little clueless, but not at all turned off.

Bed Rumors

Do women tell their friends the truth about how a guy is in bed?
—ERIC, BY E-MAIL

Of course. What's the point of talking about sex if you aren't telling the truth? When we confess carnal activities to our friends, it isn't because we're looking for an excuse to talk dirty. It's because we can't contain ourselves—the man we're dating is either so incredibly good, or so bad or bizarre that we have to tell someone about it to boast or get some advice, or at least to secure some commiseration. For example, a close friend recently turned to me at a bar and said, "This guy is so good at finding my G-spot that I can't break up with him even though he's boring as hell! What do I do?" We spent half the night trying to figure out whether some fantastic sex was worth hours of bland conversation (the answer turned out to be "Yes, but only once a week"). So, absolutely, we kiss and tell. Not to put any pressure on you, Eric.

Joy's in the Hood

Does sex feel better for a woman when the man isn't wearing a condom? —ANONYMOUS

On a purely physical level, sex always feels better when a guy isn't wearing latex over his Longfellow. But considering what's at risk without a condom—everything from genital warts to unwanted pregnancy—the worry brought on by unprotected play could ruin even the most fantastic skin-on-skin experience. So when it comes to casual sex, a condom actually ends up being the more pleasurable option because it allows us to focus on what's happening rather than on thoughts of "what if?"

Driving Her Wild

Tell me the truth: Do bigger penises really feel that much better?
—DAVE A., FT. LAUDERDALE, FLORIDA

Dirk Diggler members are like Dolly Parton knockers—sure, they sell magazines, but in reality they're much more than any one person wants or knows what to do with. Even my most oversexed female friends agree that size matters only if the organ in question is way too big (think standard-issue flashlight) or way too small (think standard-issue stogie) to be of any use. Vaginas, in case you didn't know, will expand or contract to fit what's inside them, which explains why a tiny tampon will stay put even after childbirth. Aesthetically speaking, like breasts, penises of all shapes and sizes can provide the same amount of pleasure (yes, even ones that hang serious left or right)—especially when attached to a man who has a lot more going for him than a killer unit.

For more honest answers about women, look for Ask the Men's Health *Girl Next Door wherever books are sold.*

2

MYSTERIES OF WOMEN

The idea of a "War of the Sexes " is about as outdated as the Cold War. In another time, maybe courtship was akin to spy games. But today, men and women are like two peace-loving countries negotiating free trade: Even when the talks get heated, the eventual outcome is security, prosperity, and a whole lotta intercourse.

Of course, some basic differences between men and women are older than war itself. But if you take the time to listen to and understand your mate, your diplomacy will earn you significant bedroom reparations. To learn more about becoming a successful ambassador, keep reading.

Secret Seductress

27 covert female signs that scream
"I want you!" BY LISA JONES

1. I call you by your first name instead of your nickname, because, babe, I'm not one of your buds, and I don't intend to become one.

2. I apply lip gloss often, but not in your presence. (If you witness makeup application of any sort, start calling yourself Chandler—you're officially a friend.)

3. I rub my lips together often in your presence.

4. I sit at the edge of my seat.

5. It's my birthday, and I'm still talking to you 10 minutes after you bought me a drink. (Note: Birthday girls of any age are easy—doubly so at decade markers.)

6. Instead of merlot, I order a Corona, which, conveniently, is served in a bottle—the better to sexily sip from.

7. My speech pattern is starting to resemble, like, Kirsten Dunst's.

8. You smoke. I don't. Yet I'm talking to you.

9. I touch you (for any reason) more than once.

10. I laugh, frequently and nervously, even amid humorless conversation.

11. I shout in your ear, because "it's so loud in here, I can't hear you!"

12. I use your name often in conversation.

13. I tell you that you look like some particular celebrity, which means I think both you and the celebrity are very hot.

14. I bring up antimatter and black holes, or any other such pseudo-brainy and vaguely sexual topic for discussion.

15. The place is a rod-fest, yet I'm talking to you and you alone.

16. My cell phone rings and I don't answer it. And I turn off my ringer immediately.

17. I say in a quasi–questioning/observational tone, "Your girlfriend must really like that?!" (This is a classic fishing tactic to learn whether there's currently a woman with this title in your life.)

18. I tell you you're talented. a) It's a measured remark, so you know I'm sincere; and b) by the Mick Jagger Laws of Chemistry, it must therefore follow that I think you're damn sexy. Talent is personality salsa: it adds hot to any dish.

19. I call you first. Or, sometimes, I simply call you at all.

20. When you take me out for drinks, I'm wearing a different outfit or shoes or carrying a different handbag than when you saw me earlier today.

21. I'm late, but, interestingly, I had enough time to put on mascara.

22. I tell you about the new Coldplay album, developments in the Pinochet case, or the new limited-release Dave Eggers novel I "just happened to hear about" because last time we spoke, you mentioned your interest in the London music scene, international law, or postmodern literature.

23. I ask you if you know where the coatroom/bathroom/VIP room in this place is. When you tell me, I raise my eyebrows, turn, and walk in the correct direction.

24. I'm in the bathroom for more than 3 minutes, which is always more than enough time to actually pee.

25. I ask if you want a taste of my dinner, meaning I'm willing to share more than my gnocchi.

26. You've taken over the starring role in all my fantasies. You have no way of detecting this, but I just thought you'd like to know. . . .

27. I remove any article of clothing other than my coat.

"Honey, Can I Ask You a Question?"

Ha! With women, there are no simple questions—
and even fewer answers. But follow our advice and you
can escape her seven most-cunning traps.

BY SARAH MILLER

YOU'VE SUSPECTED FOR A LONG TIME that women set traps for you. Some traps seem designed to pull you further into a relationship than you intended to go. Others seem simply to test whether or not you're on your toes. And still others—your least favorite—seem especially designed to prove what you already know: Your life is one long episode of a game show called You Can't Win! in which you play the role of hopeful contestant and women play the eternally head-shaking hosts.

What all traps have in common is that you start the day thinking everything is just fine and then suddenly find yourself in a big fight, in big trouble, or perhaps moving into an apartment with a big pink rug shaped like a heart.

Why do women set traps? Because you don't tell us anything, so we're always thinking up ingenious new methods to find out how you feel. We set traps because we're a little nuts, but not so nuts that we can't create a situation to see if you love us enough to read our minds.

Traps are sneaky, but they're not foolproof, fool. If you know where to look for traps and can spot their clever camouflaging, the relationship forest becomes much less dark and frightening. Of course, it won't be possible to avoid all of them, but even when you find yourself pinned under the metaphorical pressurized spring, you don't have to start chewing off your own limb to set yourself free.

EVIL TRAP #1: "I DON'T WANT ANYTHING FOR MY BIRTHDAY/ OUR ANNIVERSARY/INSERT ANY GIFT-FOCUSED HOLIDAY HERE"

POTENTIAL LOCATION OF TRAP: A Sunday drive, a leisurely dinner, a stroll by a lake full of swans, when you're too busy gazing into each other's eyes to notice the bird droppings or the stink. Or any moment when you're feeling like, gee, things sure are going swell.

FEMININE WILES EMPLOYED TO DISGUISE THIS TRAP: If it's set correctly, the untrained man will come upon this trap and mistake it for a loving gesture: She's letting you know that she loves you for you, not for the 2-carat butterfly diamond earrings you might buy from the jewelry store next to China Garden that she oohs and ahs over when you're full of moo goo gai pan.

DAMNED IF YOU DO: Let's say you take her at her word. You have not, as you may believe, followed her wishes. You have instead failed to reward her with a gift for her admirable lack of interest in getting a gift.

DAMNED IF YOU DON'T: Failing to believe her dismally obvious lie,

---

INSTANT SEXPERT

Moody Blues

It's easy enough to tell when your partner is in the mood. She starts playing Sting albums. But when she's not in the mood? Don't take it personally. After all, transient lack of sexual interest is rarely a sign that her lust for you has turned to loathing. She may simply not feel sexy, and the reason could have nothing to do with you. The best thing to do is accept her answer with an air of Zenlike inevitability. Hold her, kiss her, and say something like "I'll take a raincheck, then." One night soon, you'll be glad you did.

you buy her the diamond earrings. She protests that she didn't ask for these and accuses you of trying to get too serious and buying her affections. The balance of power in the relationship shifts abruptly over to her.

AVOID THE TRAP: This trap is clearly the work of a woman with serious latchkey-child issues. Mommy the power attorney didn't pay enough attention to her when she was growing up. She wants to put you in a position to let her down just like Mommy did, or to try to win her affections with bribes, just like Mommy did. For obvious reasons, you don't want to be Mommy. A woman who takes the time to tell you she doesn't want a gift is basically saying to you, "Prove your love to me, and mean it." Fortunately for you, the best gift to give someone like this is lots of sex, preferably the kind where you do a lot and she does very little.

EVIL TRAP #2: "WHAT DO YOU THINK ABOUT YOUR FRIEND JOE'S ATTITUDE TOWARD WOMEN?"

POTENTIAL LOCATION OF TRAP: In the car, while driving through one of the seedier parts of town, where your friend Joe spends most of his free time.

WHY YOU MIGHT NOT SEE IT: She will ask this question with chirpy, cheerleaderish curiosity. She's just making conversation! She's just asking you what's going on in your head, shooting the breeze! She just saw that giant neon woman with the blinking nipples, and hey, she thought of Joe and wanted to know what you thought!

FALL ON THE SHARP SIDE OF THE SWORD: Part of you thinks you should defend your buddy and say something like, "Gee, where does Joe find the time to be such a totally stand-up guy and keep the porn industry in business?" However, you know that failing to point out Joe's moral shortcomings could raise questions about your own.

FALL ON THE OTHER SHARP SIDE: Clearly, this is an opportunity to tell your girlfriend how despicable you find Joe's behavior and to point out just how far it is from your own. Well, yes, it's also an opportunity to ensure that the next time you want to go over and watch the play-offs on Joe's big-screen TV, she'll be able to shake her head and say, "I don't know why you hang out with someone you don't even respect."

AVOID THE TRAP: Say something like, "Gee, it sure does upset me how Joe thinks of nothing but fornicating with women he doesn't re-spect. Seems like every time we hang out I'm trying to get him to see the error of his ways. Sure am glad the good Lord's given me the op-portunity to lead a lost lamb like Joe into the pasture of righteousness." If you make it clear that you love the sinner and hate the sin, you will get to keep seeing Joe . . . and keep sleeping with your girlfriend.

EVIL TRAP #3: "DO YOU THINK I AM FAT/LOOK FAT/HAVE GAINED WEIGHT?" (NOTE: THIS IS THE TRAP FROM WHICH ALL OTHERS SPRING)

POTENTIAL LOCATION OF TRAP: Be especially alert when she's get-ting ready for an event—a wedding (likely of a really hot friend), a high-school reunion, or a job interview. You're also likely to encounter this trap before sex (or, if you're not careful, what was going to be sex).

FEMININE WILES EMPLOYED TO DISGUISE TRAP: There's currently no feminine wile available to disguise the nakedly abject nature of such a query.

INTO THE FRYING PAN: You might think telling her she's put on a few pounds is a good idea. After all, she'll lose a little weight and trust that you're honestly looking out for her health and best interests. Sadly, this fantasy is about as likely to come true as your coming home from work today to find redheaded triplets having a whipped-cream fight on your bed. Here's the reality: She will get very frosty and ask for specifics. Are her thighs fat? Her ass? When did you first notice? She will withhold sex for a long time. And she won't lose any weight, because—and boys, this is a promise—the only time women ever suc-ceed in losing weight is when they're single or fixing to dump you.

INTO THE FIRE: Say, "No, I think you look fine," and you're equally screwed. Because if that's what you think, you clearly don't even notice her. Worse, you may be accused of lying because you still want to get laid, even by a whale, which, if you cared at all, you would clearly see she is.

AVOID THE TRAP: When she asks you this question, make a face that reflects epic shock and disbelief. Imagine you've opened your door and not only is Ed McMahon standing there with an oversize check, he's standing there in full leather. Not only is it impossible to fathom how she could think she's fat, but you can't imagine how a being as delicate and slight as she has been able to summon the energy to speak.

ADDITIONAL HAZARDS: Under no circumstances should you reply, "I don't know, have you weighed yourself?" You might as well say, "Well, it's obvious you're a heifer. Let's talk numbers."

EVIL TRAP #4: "SO, WHAT'S YOUR FAVORITE SEX POSITION?"

POTENTIAL LOCATION OF TRAP: In bed, in the snuggly glow following rapturous carnal union. What could go wrong here?

SHOOT YOURSELF IN THE FOOT: You like it all, but hey, you're a guy. If you were about to go before the firing squad, you tell her, your last meal would be a steak and your last lay would be doggy-style. She fixes you with a wry smile and counters, "So, you can pretty much fantasize about anybody when you can't see my face, right?"

Be careful not to respond by saying, "That's not true, Selma . . . I mean, Ashley."

SHOOT YOURSELF IN THE OTHER FOOT: You rightly suspect that replying "doggy-style" is going to land you in the pound. So you say the next thing that pops into your mind: the missionary position. Surely, you can't be faulted for loyalty to an old standby! Ah, but you can! Because there she goes, getting all pouty and whining, "You don't think I'm sexy enough to be wild in bed! And I'll bet you love it when you don't have to look at my body, because then you can pretend I'm someone else."

AVOID THE TRAP: The trick here is to think for a long time, with a faraway smile on your face to indicate that you're daydreaming about your many rapturous sexual interludes with her. Then tell her you like everything, but you just happened to be thinking about her on top, where you can see her face and her body.

EVIL TRAP #5: "WHY DON'T YOU STAY WITH ME A WHILE UNTIL YOU GET A NEW PLACE?"

POTENTIAL LOCATION OF TRAP: Outside of where you lived up until a few minutes ago, when you were evicted, or there was a fire, or your buddy's new girlfriend turned your bedroom into a yoga studio.

FEMININE WILES EMPLOYED TO DISGUISE TRAP: A home-cooking-size portion of motherly concern for your safety and well-being, with a side of seduction. "Why would you want to sleep alone in a Motel 6 and cook ramen every night in your hot pot when you could eat the nice food I make for you and sleep [get laid] in my nice bed?" By the way, she's confident that this whole "when you get a new place" thing will soon become a distant memory.

SIX OF ONE: We think the downside of saying, "Sure, what the hell, just until I get a place," is obvious. If you move in with her, you'll be living together. Statistically, the odds are good that this will be a complete nightmare.

HALF A DOZEN OF THE OTHER: If you refuse this generous offer in your time of need, she'll be hurt. She'll know that you're willing to sacrifice comfort for independence, which immediately casts you in the role of suspicious character.

AVOID THE TRAP: Men, you want to be really, really careful about winding up homeless while in the midst of a relationship that's not necessarily ready to go to the cohabitation stage. The specter of moving in versus not moving in will force your commitment issues to the front row, when you'd really prefer to leave them up in the nose-bleed seats.

So when you say no—and you will say no—you must stress that it's not because you don't want to move in, but because when you move in you want to do it right. After which you must spend no more than four nights in a row (but no fewer than three!) at her place. That's just about long enough to let her know that you're potentially ready to commit, but not so much that you should contribute to the rent.

EVIL TRAP #6: "DO YOU THINK SHE'S PRETTY?"

POTENTIAL LOCATION OF TRAP: Varied. You can pretty much expect it at a wedding or a party—any event where lots of women (who have all made a special effort to look fetching) are gathered in one place. However, a woman doesn't need special circumstances to compare herself to other women or to check in on your potential impulse to do so.

Caution! This trap may be mixed in with a series of other questions ("Do you like the canapés?" "Isn't it a lovely day?" "Does your cummerbund feel okay?") to lull you into a series of answers ("Delicious." "Yes, lovely." "Yes, but these suspenders are giving me a wedgie."). By the time she gets to "Do you think she's pretty?" you could find yourself blithely replying, "I'd nail her in a heartbeat!"

INSTANT SEXPERT

Foreign Affairs

The popular notion that Eskimos rub noses as a form of intimacy is not quite accurate. In truth, they place their noses and mouths against each other's cheeks in order to smell each other.

UP AGAINST A ROCK: If you admit to finding someone attractive, you're going to spend the entire night telling people, "I'd love to introduce you to my girlfriend, but she's glowering at me from behind a fern."

UP AGAINST A HARD PLACE: If you say no every time, your girl-friend is going to suspect that you're lying. She's going to think that every girl you see inhabits some fantasy in your brain that's too raunchy to even contemplate.

AVOID THE TRAP: Many sensible, worldly women are still naive enough to believe this one: "She's, you know, definitely objectively attractive, but she's not really my type." You're admitting that you looked, and then looked away. Your girlfriend will be busy thinking to herself, "God, my man is so sweet! He really wants only me!" While she's distracted by this lunacy, you're free to imagine what the woman in question would look like crawling around naked in a giant tub of oil.

ADDITIONAL HAZARDS: "Which of my friends do you think is pretty?" There's a little tiny part of you that actually believes answering this question truthfully could land you in a hot threesome. That little tiny part of you is so stupid that you should probably kill it if you think there will be enough of you left to survive.

EVIL TRAP #7: YOUR EXCLUSIVE (AS FAR AS YOU KNOW, UP TO THIS POINT) GIRLFRIEND ASKS, "DO YOU THINK WE SHOULD SEE OTHER PEOPLE?"

WHY SHE'LL CLAIM SHE'S ASKED THIS: Because she really cares about your relationship and doesn't want you to move too quickly and ruin a good thing. Because she likes you a lot, but doesn't want you to feel like you're "owned."

POSSIBLE REAL REASON: She wants to place in your mind the image of her having sex with another man, which will, undoubtedly, result in a dramatic declaration of your love.

ANOTHER POSSIBLE REAL REASON: She's pretty sure you're interested in someone else and wants to see how many milliseconds elapse before you say, "What a great idea." Then you two can have a big fight, which will, if you want it to end, require a dramatic declaration of your love.

YET ANOTHER POSSIBLE REAL REASON: She wants to see someone else and blame you when she strays.

VARIATIONS ON THIS TRAP THAT YOU COULD FIND YOURSELF IN DEPENDING ON THE MOTIVES THAT MAY OR MAY NOT BE IN PLAY: This is an extremely tricky trap because you can never be entirely sure why she's asking.

You don't want to be too eager to say yes, because if she's testing your loyalty, you could end up playing the field with no nice, warm dugout to come home to. You also don't want to refuse too quickly, because if she does have her eye on someone, she's likely to investigate with or without your consent. You might as well be officially free to do the same. Finally, if you're totally smitten with her, and the very idea of "other people" makes you want to chug Maalox, you probably want to keep that to yourself, too. Once you reveal desperation and anxiety over possible competition, you've already lost. She may think she wants a declaration of love, but just like men, women get a lot less interested when they know they have your undivided attention.

AVOID THE TRAP: "Do you want to see other people?" is such an obvious invitation to go into a jealous fit that you can only respond one way: with the kind of composure that makes Clint Eastwood look like Halle Berry accepting her Oscar. A slow, easy shrug will go nicely with whatever you say, which should be something like, "I don't want to own you, baby, I just want to be with you." Smile warmly when you say this. Touch her shoulder, or even her cheek. Now she's the one freaking out. And you, my friend, are as cool as a cucumber. Let freedom ring.

The Sexual Aptitude Test

You've been studying women your whole life. Now it's time
to take our SAT and see how you score.

BY SARAH MILLER

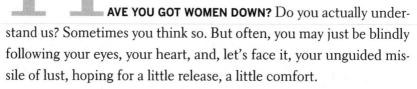

HAVE YOU GOT WOMEN DOWN? Do you actually understand us? Sometimes you think so. But often, you may just be blindly
following your eyes, your heart, and, let's face it, your unguided mis-
sile of lust, hoping for a little release, a little comfort.

Now you can finally put an end to that never-ending question—
How well do I really know women?—by taking our SAT (Sexual Aptitude Test).

This series of 13 relatively simple questions looks at everything
from the first meeting to sex, from serious relationships to breakups.
It measures the extent of your knowledge and highlights different relationship phases to determine your areas of strength and weakness.
Best of all, it results in an actual score, which you can either brag
about or be quietly ashamed of.

Don't put down the book and run off to cram. You've had years,
perhaps decades, to prep for this, and either that time has been pro-
ductive or it hasn't. Knowledge—even if that knowledge is that you're
a total moron—is power. Don't hesitate. Do grab a beer and a
number-two pencil.

SECTION I: INTRODUCTIONS

1. You met Wendy at a bar, at a bar mitzvah, in baggage claim, whatever, we don't care. The point is that the extremely hot Wendy is per-

haps slightly out of your league, but not so far that you lack hope. Besides, in your best moments, you recall that Wendy seemed interested. Right now, Wendy is probably thinking . . .

A. "That guy was kind of cute. I wonder what I'll wear when we go out. . . ."

B. "I hope he calls me. He won't. God, I wonder if he thought he liked me and then saw how fat my ass is and changed his mind. Maybe he likes me. But maybe he's too cute for me?"

C. "I am so hot. So many guys approach me. I wish they'd just give up."

D. About something other than you.

The correct answer is B. We aren't going to sign an affidavit swearing that Wendy wants you, but if she acted interested, she probably was. The point is, when it comes to love and attraction, women (even really pretty ones—especially really pretty ones) are just as terrified, insecure, and self-doubting as you are. We are not the cold, arrogant, oblivious creatures that you fear. Well, at least not most of the time.

2. It's Saturday night, and you find yourself—gee, who'da thunk it?—in a loud, crowded bar. You spot a female you think might make a wonderful companion—for an evening, for a lifetime . . . who can say? The line most likely to get you in there is . . .

A. "If I said you had a beautiful body, would you hold it against me?"

B. "Hi, I just wanted to introduce myself. I'm [say your name]. And you are?"

C. "Hi: I just wanted to tell you I think you're really pretty."

D. No line, because lines aren't cool.

The correct answer is C. Option A is the work of a man whose charming self-deprecation permits him to poke fun at himself for having no game. Sadly, what we take away isn't so much the charming self-deprecation thing as the having-no-game thing. As for B—sweetheart, "introduce" has three syllables. This is a bar, not *As Schools Match Wits*. If you answered D, you're definitely cool. You are also definitely taking off your own pants tonight. It's all about C: direct, sexy, confident. A girl who's in a bar on a Saturday night doesn't want to hear anything else. Absolute worst-case scenario: You get a smile and a thank-you. You know what absolute best is.

SECTION II: DATING, PRESEX

3. In your first extended private conversation, the best way to distinguish yourself as the man she wants is to . . .

> **A.** Tell lots of really funny stories.
> **B.** Ask about her mom, her cat, her college major, her job, her deflowering. . . .
> **C.** Search for things you have in common that you can discuss.
> **D.** Avoid all topics you know nothing about, which means letting her do most of the talking while you nod knowingly.

It's B. Women do value a sense of humor (A), but as a dating routine, funny stories come across as self-promoting. C isn't bad, either, but it works best for a first meeting; the search for common ground can be exhausting and repetitive. (Yep, empanadas. Yep, I like 'em, too. Chicken ones. Yep. Tennis. Love it. Great. Yep.) You can't go wrong by peppering a chick with questions. Feel free to start with the innocuous stuff and slowly get dirty. ("Where did you get your socks?" "Do you have fluorescent stars over your bed?" "How do you feel about threesomes?") As for D—we know you love the path of least resistance, but there'll be plenty of time for that once you start dating.

4. The correct number of flowers to bring to a woman the first time you bring flowers is . . .

A. 1
B. 2
C. 5
D. 12

The answer is C. One flower suggests you haven't had sex since your prom. Two is a hint that you stole them from someone's porch on the way over. Five is perfect. Giving her five flowers advertises you as a man of restraint and taste—polite, generous, but not overeager. A dozen? Try that only if you want to be confused with the last three losers she dated.

SECTION III: DATING, WITH SEX

5. Male sex drive is to female sex drive, as . . .

A. Apple is to orange
B. Bulldozer is to tricycle
C. Corvette is to Aston Martin
D. Snake is to quivering mouse

The answer is C. A suggests that the male and female sex drives bear no relation to each other—clearly misguided. B implies that the male sex drive far overpowers the female—an old myth, as is the predator-prey relation of D. Only C works. An Aston Martin can keep up with a Corvette, but it builds its reputation on elegance and subtlety, not on drag racing.

6. If x equals the number of men she told you she's slept with and y equals the actual number, then x/y is . . .

A. 1 (she told you the truth)
B. Greater than 1 (she rounded up)
C. Less than 1 (she rounded down)
D. A lot less than 1 (she rounded way down)

The answer is C. Unless female promiscuity miraculously becomes a virtue, no woman is going to exaggerate her number of sex partners or even acknowledge the true number. We would like to lie to you—that's D—and present ourselves as virgins, but we are planning to eventually relate to you every last anecdote from our past romances. And if we admitted to having sex with six guys but told you stories about, say, 60, you'd, uh, sniff us out. Only C keeps things real, but not too real.

SECTION IV: COUPLEHOOD

7. It's time for the First Significant Gift for a Significant Woman. The most appropriate gift is . . .

> **A.** New stereo speakers ($200 or so), because she really needs them
> **B.** A weekend away at a nice hotel
> **C.** Expensive jewelry ($400 or more)
> **D.** Inexpensive jewelry ($200 or less)

It's D. Sure, C makes a big statement, maybe big enough to scare her, or you. Practicality (A) is thoughtful but not sexy. B is sexy, but the gift should be for her, not for both of you. D—a handmade silver ring or a pair of nice earrings—is a way to play your cards right without laying them all on the table.

8. You like to have sex doggy-style. She likes it, too, but nowhere near as much as you do. How many non–doggy-style encounters should occur before you request doggy-style again?

> **A.** 0
> **B.** 2
> **C.** 15
> **D.** 30

The answer is A, and yes, this is a trick question. What, pray tell, would you be doing requesting things in bed? Women don't think of bed as a place for polite inquiries; it's a place where you get us so turned on, you're not asking, we're begging. Ruff, ruff.

SECTION V: SERIOUS COUPLEHOOD

9. It's very obvious to you, not being blind or deaf, that your long-term (1 year plus) girlfriend has a crush on a male friend. You like this woman and don't feel like losing her to this bozo, who just happens to have a six-pack, a lot of money, and a great personality. Assuming you and your girlfriend have a good relationship, the strategy most likely to keep you in and Bozo out involves . . .

A. Doing nothing.

B. Embarking on a serious regimen of self-improvement. You have a six-pack and a fortune waiting to be made as well. They're just hiding under a thin layer of beer, tuna melts, and lethargy.

C. Beating your girlfriend to the punch and suggesting you see other people.

D. Letting your girlfriend know that you've noticed her little case of wandering eye and you'd prefer that she and Bozo weren't friends.

> **INSTANT SEXPERT**
> ## Pickup and Roll
> The good news: Pickup lines really can work. The bad news: Yours don't. Why not try an opening line instead? The latter is a sincere, fairly spontaneous expression of interest in the woman at hand. The former is a rehearsed script that you trot out (usually with accompanying lounge lizard persona) for every last woman. A line like "Hey, baby, buy a drunken idiot a drink?" leaves her only two possible answers: "No" and "Hell, no."

A is not only the best strategy; it's the only strategy. C is tempting, but understand that a woman with a sexual crush is just as shameless as a man—give her permission to see Bozo and before long she'll be walking around naked with a big red ball on her nose. The impulse to make yourself over, B, is misguided—she's not dreaming of a new you; she's dreaming, as you sometimes do, of novelty. You might believe D is your right. But remember this: Demanding fidelity, especially when the demand stems from insecurity, is the best way not to get it. Threats to your relationship are everywhere, but they lose a lot of their power when you ignore them.

10. Let *x* represent a woman's age and let *y* represent the amount of crap she'll put up with from you once it's clearly established that you like each other. A graph representing the relationship between these two things will look like . . .

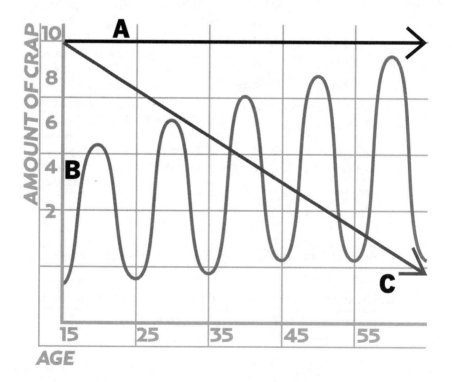

I'd love to say that either B or C is the answer. It would be nice if there were at least some point in a woman's life at which she would cease to tolerate your lack of consideration and your general idiocy. But, sadly, if she's into you, it doesn't matter if she's 18 or 80, she'll put up with just about any crap you can sling until, as shown in A, the day one of you drops dead.

11. During a fight, your girlfriend launches an assault on your personality in a way that's both meticulously detailed and very loud. When it's your turn to speak, the absolute worst response you can give is . . .

A. "I'm incredibly uncomfortable right now, and I wish I were somewhere else."
B. "I'd be willing to accept the fact that I am the world's biggest jerk, but I really think that award might go to you. Let me tell you why. . . . "
C. "I don't know what to say."
D. "You're cute when you get mad."

The answer is C. Next time you "don't know what to say," remember that you're much better off with lame honesty (A) or even cruel retaliation (B). Both show at least scant evidence of the thought and self-awareness infuriatingly absent from C, six words that confirm our worst fear: that you have no capacity for or interest in sharing your emotions and that you wish women would miraculously disappear and be reincarnated as mute models balancing big-screen TVs on our heads and bearing cold beer and cigars. D was included only to show the total unacceptability of C and is also probably not a good idea.

SECTION VI: BREAKUPS

12. You've been dating a woman for 2 months. Assume that there's no one else and you want out because you're not into her anymore. The best reason you can give is . . .

A. "There's someone else."

B. "I'm just not as sexually attracted to you as I thought I was."

C. "I'm still in love with my ex-girlfriend."

D. "I don't think I'm capable of offering the kind of intimacy you deserve."

The answer is A. Anyone who's dumped knows deep down that the reason why is always some simple variation on B, which, unfortunately, is too cruel a thing to say. However, C and D are even crueler, because women, nursed on soap operas and Danielle Steele paperbacks, hear them as rays of poignant romantic hope. "There's someone else" might be a lie, but it's also the only breakup language women seem to understand. Please learn to speak it.

13. You live in New York City and met Denise, who lives in St. Louis, at a wedding in Miami. You got drunk, went back to her hotel room, and took things from there. A month later, Denise is in New York and you have sex once more, but the thrill is gone. You tell her you think you'd be better as friends. Next thing you know, Denise is in New York for 3 months on business and sees you as her personal tour guide. You have an obligation to . . .

    A. Screen Denise's calls repeatedly until she gets the message.

    B. Make sure Denise is thoroughly entertained when she's in town. It's only 3 months. And you did have sex. Twice.

    C. Invite Denise along to parties—maybe she'll like one of your friends.

    D. Sit Denise down and explain to her that you had a really great time at the wedding and you're sorry things didn't work out. You have your life and she has hers, and you wish her the best but don't have time to invest in her.

It's A. Nothing says "Leave me alone" like unanswered calls. Denise needs to take care of Denise, and neither B nor C will create the correct environment for her to do so. D gets the point across, but in an unnecessarily belabored manner—besides, if that's the conversation she craves, she should have had a one-night stand with Dr. Phil.

SCORING

Unlike the SAT you took in high school, in which a score of 1600 was tops, you're shooting for a 130. Give yourself 10 points for each correct answer.

90–130: Nice job. You show an impressive mastery of one of the most mysterious, unknowable creations in the history of evolution. If women were colleges, you'd get into all of them.

50–80: You, unlike the guys with the 90–130 scores, are looking at safety schools. Think about where you got most of your wrong answers. Maybe lots of women are interested in you, but you have trouble taking things to the next level. Or maybe you're great once conversations start, but not so great at making opportunities to talk one-on-one. Either way, you've got enough strength to build on once you identify your weaknesses.

Less than 50: We suspect that you enrolled in women's studies but were too enraptured with the eye candy to take notes. The bad news is that the motivations and machinations of half of the world's population make absolutely no sense to you. The good news is that free, private tutoring is available.

Body of Evidence

Her tattoos thrill you. Her tongue stud chills you.
But what do her "accessories" really say about her?
Use this handy guide to enjoy the ride.

BY JOE KITA

A
S IF THE FEMALE BODY weren't alluring enough, an increasing number of women are adorning it with all kinds of intriguing stuff—tattoos, belly rings, tongue studs, body glitter, elaborate manicures . . . you name it.

The trend has nothing to do with honesty; it's about advertising," says Helen Fisher, Ph.D., an anthropologist at Rutgers University, in New Jersey. "Courtship is all about display. And if there was ever a time when women needed to display themselves, it's now. For hundreds of years we lived in small social units where everybody knew everyone else. But these days women move around a lot, and as a result, they're looking for any little thing to catch the eye of the right guy. As Mae West said, 'It is better to be looked over than overlooked.'"

What follows is a cheat sheet. We asked relationship and body-art experts to generalize about the type of woman who decorates herself in these ways. Take a long look. She's sending signals without even opening her mouth. Pay attention and you'll be that much closer to figuring her out.

A SMALL TATTOO ON A WOMAN'S SHOULDER means she's funny and overtly sexy and loves to tease, according to Amy Krakow, author of *Total Tattoo Book*. This woman wants something unexpected and memorable to catch your eye when she wheels on her heels, throws you a coquettish smile, and takes leave. "Invite her out for a night of dancing, preferably Latin dancing," suggests Krakow. "And don't forget to kiss the tattoo. The shoulder is a very erotic spot."

A TATTOO ON THE SMALL OF THE BACK suggests a woman who is secretly sexual. The sacrum is an overlooked but highly sensual spot where most women love to be touched. She's essentially telling you to "press here." This type of tattoo, especially if it's a tribal design, also connotes spirituality and a wider perspective on reality. "Bring her aromatherapy candles," says Krakow, "and be sure to ask what her tattoo means. Lower-back tattoos are usually very personal."

DIFFERENT LIPSTICK SHADES mean different things. According to Michael Cunningham, Ph.D., a psychologist at the University of Louisville, a lady in red is obviously passionate. Get tangled up with her and you'll be buying Tide in bulk. Light pink connotes a cooler, more aloof gal, who's in charge of herself and potentially of you. Colorless high-gloss, the kind that makes lips look wet, suggests a woman who is sensual but receptive. Play it right with her and you'll stick.

IF HER EYELINER CURVES UP AT THE CORNERS, she wants to be seen as mysterious, exotic, and divine. The look harks back to Nefertiti, a beautiful Egyptian queen who probably made herself up like this to resemble the cats her people worshiped. So we're talking wannabe diva here. Either be prepared to adore her, or ignore her.

A BICEPS BRACELET OR AN ARMBAND TATTOO signifies toughness. According to Krakow, a woman with body art on a typically male place of adornment, such as the forearm or biceps, is willing to stand up for herself and won't take any crap. Better not insult her. Since she's calling attention to that arm, she probably works out.

AN EYEBROW RING OR ANY OTHER UNCONVENTIONAL FACIAL PIERCING is there for shock value. "Novelty raises levels of dopamine in the male brain," says Fisher. "This hormone is associated with romantic love, and it heightens sex drive." So what you have here is a rebel—a girl of brassy independence who likes to be provocative and occasionally make trouble. If you catch her eye, do nothing. Before long, she'll be over to ask you out.

A SMALL TATTOO ON HER PUBIC BONE OR ATOP HER BREAST may indicate she's coming off a bad relationship. "Some women, especially older ones, get tattooed in private places to reassert ownership of their bodies," says Krakow. A sun design or a butterfly may represent her desire to rise again and be free. To win her broken heart, do just one thing: Listen.

A TINY TATTOO ON THE ANKLE signifies a good girl who wants to be bad. She probably works in a professional environment that frowns on tats, so she picked one that's less likely to be noticed. A rose symbolizes love and romance. An angel represents protection. Fairies connote nature and magic. A dolphin is phallic. And twin cherries, well, you can only imagine. Buy her a few drinks and let her sassy side emerge. And keep in mind that any woman with a tattoo likes a little pain with her pleasure. Says Krakow, "Getting a tattoo on a place with no body fat, like the ankle, hurts more. But it's sensuous pain—the warmth of the needle and the sting." Looks like it's your lucky day, pal—finally, a girl who doesn't mind pricks.

BODY GLITTER: If she's wearing body glitter or crystals, she wants to sparkle just like they do. She's girlish and fun, curious and playful, and she still believes in magic. In fact, she's looking for a Prince Charming to put some real twinkle on her finger. Might be you. But check to be sure she's legal first. Teenagers love this stuff.

TONGUE STUDS are the most in-your-face pieces of body art a woman can have, obviously done to enhance oral sex. "This is a self-confident woman who values her tongue almost as much for sex as for talking," says Cunningham. But there's more to it than just fabulous fellatio. The tongue has loads of nerve endings, so it's the most painful body part to pierce. Plus, the risk of infection is high, and the stud compromises language skills, at least at first. In this respect, it's sort of like the peacock's tail. "It's saying, 'I have so much energy and am in such good health that I can cart around this cumbersome thing, yet still function,'" says Fisher. "It's a big fitness indicator." In other words, this gal can lick you in more ways than one. Be careful.

BELLY ART calls attention to a woman's stomach. A navel ring, a belly chain, or a small tattoo send the signal that she's sexual, fertile, and possibly ready to reproduce. Men don't just size up potential mates by their facial features. We subconsciously weigh a multitude of factors, including waist-to-hip ratio. The ideal ratio for childbearing is 0.7, which equates to the classic hourglass shape of a 27-inch waist and 38-inch hips. So if she's got it and she's flaunting it, she's probably the type who wants to have kids—maybe not immediately, but someday. In the meantime, let her call you baby.

NOSE PIERCING: A stud in the side of the nose means this woman is worldly and a little exotic. "It's a common decoration in India and other cultures," says Cunningham. Take her to dinner at an ethnic restaurant, and then see a foreign film. Mention that you have relatives in Burma. (Do not, at any time, offer her a tissue.)

EAR PIERCINGS, in multiples, mean that a woman can't get enough of a good thing. "If one is attractive, then two has to be twice as attractive, and six has to be an order of magnitude above that," says Cunningham. This tough-to-satisfy gal may have lots of credit-card debt, a closetful of shoes, and more exes than a moonshine jug. But on the bright side, she's probably multiorgasmic.

Rockin' the Cradle

Is it wrong for a middle-aged man to date
a 20-something woman?

BY GEOFFREY JAMES

I'M **49 YEARS OLD.** Soon AARP will send me an official reminder of my imminent slide from middle age into the world of senior discounts.

Not long ago, my fiancée passed a milestone of her own: She bought her first legal alcoholic drink.

She's 21. We're getting married this summer.

I know what you're thinking: I'm some guy who left his wife and kids in a desperate attempt to recapture my youth, and my fiancée is just brainless, gold-digging eye candy looking for a sugar daddy. But it's not like that. She's intelligent, creative, and spiritual—though, yes, she happens to be beautiful. Me? I'm convinced that older man–younger woman relationships can be as healthy as, or maybe healthier than, relationships between age peers. They sure are more fun, once you learn to deal with the fact that you're violating almost everyone's idea of what a good relationship is all about.

For the past 10 years, I've declined to date seriously any woman who isn't significantly younger than I. I have my reasons, and believe it or not, sex isn't high on the list. Today's young women can be surprisingly modest. There are, of course, young women who sleep around, but they're more interested in dating a cute boy who drives a pickup than in starting a relationship with someone more mature.

I clearly remember the day I decided to date young. I was in my

Getting Back in the Game?

Singles bars and health clubs are a waste of time. Older men meet younger women in everyday settings—at weddings, bookstores, the office—where the women aren't cruising for someone their own age.

Women in their late teens and early 20s are more likely to date an older guy than women in their late 20s or early 30s. Why? The younger ones already know you're "too old" for them. The older ones aren't sure, and your overture is an uncomfortable reminder of their own age. They may resent it. If a 19-year-old thinks you're 32 and then finds out you're 42, she'll be more amused than alarmed.

Nothing turns off a young woman more quickly than an old guy on the make. Low-key and friendly is the way; enjoy the process of getting to know somebody new.

The smarter the young woman the more likely she'll go out with an older guy. My steady dates included three Ivy League students. The brighter women tend to be turned off by the relatively one-dimensional guys their age.

G.J.

late 30s (but looked younger), newly divorced (but with no kids), and hadn't seriously dated in nearly 15 years. I was walking down a muggy city street when I wound up behind three coeds wearing tight shorts.

They were achingly beautiful and, for a middle-aged guy like me, unapproachable. I felt ancient. That night, as I sat alone on my hotel bed, clicking through the movie menu, I made a decision. Somehow I was going to date the women I had wanted to date when I was younger but hadn't had the guts to ask out.

I took action. I lost the love handles, updated the wardrobe, cut the aging-hippie ponytail, dumped the old-guy eyeglasses. I'm not

(continued on page 78)

Why I'd Date an Older Man   By Lisa Jones

Given a choice between George Clooney and Prince William—two men on every most-eligible-bachelor list worldwide—I'd choose 42-year-old Clooney, pants down, over the prince who's exactly half his age. That's a bold statement, considering that William is rich, handsome, destined to be king—and about the same age as I am. But then again, I'm like a lot of young women out there: The men I should be attracted to rarely interest me. It's not that I discriminate against young guys—I'm very much an equal opportunity dater—it's just that they're guys, and what I'm looking for is a man.

Of course, age alone doesn't make a man sexy. Fact is, right around age 35, men start to fall into one of two categories: attractive bachelor or pathetic single guy. (Or, if he's married with kids: the Pat Riley DILF.) The Clooneys and Rileys of this world attract the admiring glances of younger women because they've cultivated some of these characteristics.

He's Experienced but Not Fatherly

A sexy older man has sampled enough of life to know how to success-fully navigate roadblocks. He has wisdom to share, but he's not all up in your grill about it. He doesn't even know what all up in your grill means—and that's a good thing. He's a problem-solver but doesn't try to solve his lover's troubles. He listens to her, supports her decisions, and offers his solutions if, and only if, she asks.

He's Intelligent yet Hip

He discusses the postmodern complexities of *Blade Runner* and the so-cial implications of punk rock, not the differences between seed and venture capital.

He's Successful but Not Flashy

He's a man who has something to show for his life—a career he's pas-sionate about, a home or roots of some kind, and relationships. He's invested in his life and in the world, financially and figuratively. His success is sexy; it's subtle and speaks for itself. He doesn't flaunt his possessions or use them as bait for potential lovers.

He's in Shape and Healthy

He exercises and eats healthfully, but not just for vanity's sake. He cares about his health and his future and has given up smoking and binge drinking and other early-adulthood habits. A man who takes care of himself is capable of taking care of other people—like, say, his future children.

He's Stylish but Age-Appropriate

This man has developed a classic and unique style that reflects his age and status in life. He knows the value of quality clothing and good tailoring. And he knows how to spend money well. He seems as if he'd give good gifts of elegant lingerie.

He Acknowledges His Age but Doesn't Focus on It

When he dates a younger woman, it's not because he gets off, creepy-style, on the fact that she's 22 and he's 42. He doesn't patronize her with endless conversations about the age difference.

He Makes Me Dream about Taking Him to Bed

An older man presumably has had enough sex to figure out exactly what women want in bed. He's polite and discreet. His intentions—and his ability to follow through on them—are telegraphed through a knowing twinkle in his eye, not a drunken shimmy on the dance floor.

He Knows What He Wants

He has passed the waffling what-do-I-do stage. When he wants a woman, he tells her. And not surprisingly, he often gets her.

Hollywood handsome or particularly wealthy, but I don't look like a middle-aged shlump. I take the trouble to dress in a manner that young women like. (Hint: Wear nice shoes.) More important, I changed my attitude about meeting women. Most guys feel like failures when they get shot down; I decided the real failure was in not making that first move.

Initially, I made an ass of myself. But once I learned the rules (see "Getting Back in the Game?," page 75), I dated more than a dozen young women, many of them less than half my age. What was it like?

Sometimes it was fabulous. Young women are just starting out in life. They see the world as full of adventure, excitement, and possibility. And guess what: That's the way I still feel about my life. I may be nearly 50, but I want to conquer new worlds, write great novels, paint frescoes, compose symphonies. Some "age-appropriate" women I know revel in puncturing such fantasies. Young women see me as I want to see myself: as somebody whose dreams could actually become reality. A friend of mine, a movie producer in his early 40s, put it this way, "When I'm talking to a young woman, I'm in heaven. It's not what she says; it's how she makes me feel."

Other times, it was bizarre. Young women do sometimes seem as if they're from another dimension in terms of taste and fashion. I once discovered (under the dress of a 22-year-old Irish waitress) a massive, flaming tattoo that wrapped around her entire body. Then there was a 4-hour drive to the beach (in midwinter—very romantic) with a 19-year-old fundamentalist Christian who insisted upon singing along to her favorite Barry Manilow cassette.

Sometimes it was bizarre and fabulous.

I attended a high-school prom when I was 38. I know the visual you have: creepy old guy lurking in the gymnasium, checking out the 16-year-old talent. Here's the truth: The girl who asked me to the prom was a 19-year-old political refugee who was finishing an education that had been interrupted by a bloody coup in Eastern Europe.

She wanted to experience everything the USA had to offer, including her senior prom. I was her boyfriend—we'd met by phone when she'd dialed the wrong number, and we'd talked for weeks before anything romantic developed. I got my tuxedo out of mothballs. She thought the frilly formal dresses at the local shop were ridiculous, so she sewed one herself, an ivory satin sheath right out of *Doctor Zhivago*. It was an unforgettable night.

Then there was my future wife, whom I met when she cleaned my house as part of a summer job. Tall and slender, with exotic eyes, she was just another pretty girl—until she told me she plans to teach music to kids (preferably handicapped ones) after she graduates from college. While she cleaned, I put on a tape of my father playing the piano, and we chatted about ballet and the local music scene. I gave her a copy of one of my books as she left, and she e-mailed me a few days later. We spent many hours together, walking and talking mostly, before we ever kissed.

I learned that she's an extraordinary person. She's been taught since childhood that women are men's equals, so she doesn't feel a need to prove the point. And she's easy to please. It had been a long time since anyone had thanked me for doing something simple, like taking her to a coffee shop for lunch. We got along so well that the age difference slipped into the background. We do the same things other couples do—movies, concerts, hikes—and we talk about literature, history, religion, and music.

We make plans for the future, figuring how to adapt our lives to two careers, with children on the horizon. We're a normal couple trying to live a normal life. The fact that I'm well over twice her age isn't significant—to us, at least.

Everyone else seems obsessed, especially now that we're getting married. My middle-aged friends think I'm nuts. It was one thing merely to date young; that's just middle-age crazy. But marriage and kids? And her friends were less than supportive ("Ew, he must be all wrinkly!"). We see the curious looks from men and feel the dagger stares from women. We've heard it all.

OBJECTION #1: "YOU'RE CAUSING HER TO MISS OUT ON ALL THE FUN OF BEING IN HER 20S"

Really? Would people say that to a 20-something woman who married someone her own age? The real issue is whether this is a relationship between equals. It would be highly presumptuous of me to try to make her life decisions. If my fiancée wanted the bar-hopping life of the typical Gen-Y single, she'd be hanging out at the local dance club. She evidently prefers to spend time with me.

OBJECTION #2: "WHEN YOU'RE OLD AND FEEBLE, SHE'LL STILL BE OF CHILDBEARING AGE"

I don't think so. My role model is nonagenarian bodybuilder Jack LaLanne. I fully expect to be pumping iron (and popping Viagra, if necessary) until I reach triple digits. I know couch-potato fathers in their 30s who are in far worse shape than I am. Aging is relative.

OBJECTION #3: "HER PARENTS WILL HATE THE FACT THAT YOU'RE AS OLD AS THEY ARE"

Wrong. Turns out they're less concerned about my age than about whether I'll treat their daughter with love and respect. A bonus: We have a lot in common, and I enjoy spending time with them. How many future grooms can say that?

OBJECTION #4: "YOU'RE THREATENED BY WOMEN YOUR OWN AGE WHO ARE YOUR INTELLECTUAL EQUALS"

In fact, I'm good friends with several women my age; I just don't care to date them. (And vice versa; they find me "a bit immature.") This I'll confess: I enjoy being a mentor. I'm even in the Big Brother program.

OBJECTION #5: "YOU'RE JUST A FATHER FIGURE TO HER"

So what else is new? All relationships have parental undertones; ours is out in the open. I do know this: If I tried to treat my fiancée like a daughter, she'd laugh in my face.

OBJECTION #6: "YOU'RE GOING TO DIE LONG BEFORE SHE DOES"

Okay, you got me. This bothered me so much that I almost didn't propose. But when I finally did, on a crisp autumn day by a quiet lake, leaves drifting down, she told me that she'd rather spend a few years with me than a lifetime without me.

I might have done some dumb things in my life, but I'm not going to throw away that kind of love.

As you've probably gathered, I'm convinced that I've found my soul mate. I'm so convinced, in fact, that I'd still be interested in her if she were 49, like me. When people think about us theoretically—as you are—it disturbs them. Until they see us together. Then they realize: Those two are meant to be together.

Anyway, despite the challenges we face, this middle-aged guy is going to marry his way-too-young fiancée at a big, fat, white wedding. Wish us luck.

HER CHEATIN' HEART

Here's another reason (other than the obvious) to keep track of the menstrual cycle of the woman in your life: She casts a wandering eye when she's at her most fertile. Researchers at the University of New Mexico have found that during ovulation, women tend to think about men other than their partners more than at any other time. Men sense this—we're more attentive during this time. (How do we know? Possibly it's through scent, or maybe we notice how her eyes follow the UPS man.) The researchers speculate that it's an evolutionary thing—that cavewomen might have liked the concept of different daddies to make their broods more diverse; we didn't. Still don't.

SHE'S SO VAIN

If your beautiful new girlfriend treats you like crap, it may be narcissism rearing its flawless head and gazing into the mirror. Researchers at the University of Georgia and Carnegie Mellon University, in Pennsylvania, confirmed what we learned sophomore year—and it still hurts: People with extremely high opinions of themselves aren't in relationships for intimacy. They're looking for power, status, and attention. "Narcissists can be a hell of a lot of fun," says Eli Finkel, Ph.D., a coauthor of the study. But you can't count on them for long-term love.

Warning Signs She's a Narcissist

> • She's proud to have you on her arm in public but ignores you when you're alone together.
> • She draws attention to herself and likes to have men attend to her.
> • She talks about her accomplishments a lot.
> • She thinks poorly of people who have lower-status jobs, such as waiters.

Best approach: She's a roller coaster, not Amtrak. Expect a short (exhilarating) ride, and nobody will get hurt.

TELL HER WHERE TO GO

You gave her directions, and she still got lost. She blames your directions, while you blame her.

Everybody calm down. It's biology's fault. Researchers at the University of Saskatchewan determined that men and women find their ways differently. Women tend to rely on landmarks and visual clues, while men are likely to use compass directions and distances. So instead of saying, "Go north for 2 miles and then get on Route 22 eastbound," you should tell her, "Turn left, go through three lights, and get on the ramp right after the Dunkin' Donuts. And pick me up a cruller."

FIGHTIN' WORDS

Want to win an argument with a woman? Stop trying to win. This ain't hockey, pal. "Winning an argument is an oxymoron for most couples," says Patricia Love, Ed.D., a relationship consultant and author of *The Truth about Love*. "You'll rarely get the last word with a woman, but even if you do, it doesn't mean anything if you haven't resolved the problem." What does she want? To know you're listening and understanding her point of view—which is what you want from her, too. So when you start overheating, try Love's 2-minute drill: Let her talk for 2 minutes while you listen. Now it's your turn. "You'll keep it succinct and get to the point, with no interruptions," Love says. After a few of these serve-and-volleys, she'll know you're listening, and you'll be closer to resolving your problem. Now slap hands and shower up.

> **INSTANT SEXPERT**
>
> ### Myth of the Month
>
> Uncircumcised men have better sex.
>
> False. Researchers at the Louisiana State University school of medicine studied 15 men who underwent circumcision as adults. (All together now: Ouch!) They found that there was no statistically significant difference in sex drive, erection, ejaculation, or overall satisfaction.

ASK THE GIRL NEXT DOOR

The honest truth about women from our lovely neighbor

Waiting for the Egg Timer to Ding

Why do women always make us wait for sex at the beginning of a relationship? —BOBBY, HOUSTON, TEXAS

Because we're just not programmed to hump the first thing that comes along, you included. Evolution has hardwired us to protect our eggs, to make sure that the guy we welcome into our bed is worthy. So, even though we may have no intention of making babies with you, we move slowly at first, to size you up and decide if the chemistry is right.

I can speak for, like, 99 percent of the women out there—we prefer to be thinking sweet, romantic thoughts like "Gee, I wonder what kind of movies he likes," and not "Gee, I wonder if I'm the only person he's sleeping with and whether or not he's had a recent HIV test." Besides, if we have sex after a few dates, a whole slew of awkward and premature conversations about "us" suddenly become necessary. Rookie relationships usually crumble like biscotti under that kind of pressure. On the bright side, there's the undeniable power of anticipation: The longer you wait, the more you'll want it—and so will we.

Fear Herself

What are women's biggest relationship fears?

—SIMON, ARLINGTON, VIRGINIA

Seeing an uncircumcised penis. Just kidding. We're afraid of being duped—of finding out that the man we've trusted completely has lied or cheated or both. We're afraid of being left—suddenly and without reason. We're afraid we'll want to leave—suddenly and without reason. We're afraid we'll end up old maids. We're afraid we won't be fertile when we finally want to get pregnant. Most of all, we're afraid of becoming half of an old, boring couple that doesn't crack jokes, kiss, dance, or have sex anymore.

Really Want to Know?
What are women thinking during sex?   —MARK, KANKAKEE, ILLINOIS

If you were to connect a set of speakers to a girl's brain during great
sex, you'd hear a string of X-rated sentence fragments and a lot of
static. What's coming out of our mouths in the way of moans and
squeals and "Mmmmm-yeah-do-that-baby-ooooooh-my-God!" is
pretty much shooting straight out of our frontal lobes. On the other
hand, if you tuned in during a nervous or uncomfortable encounter,
you'd hear stuff like "Ow, the stubble on his face is so rough this feels
like dermabrasion, not cunnilingus!" "Does he think I look fat?" "This
bed is too noisy, I can't concentrate. I wonder if I remembered to file
that report in the right folder. I think I'll have Mini Wheats for breakfast
instead of raisin bran." "Can he tell that last moan was fake? I wonder
why we're so off tonight. Maybe we can have sex again in the morning
to make up for it." In other words, if it's not going well, we're thinking
instead of feeling blissfully brain-dead. Not a good thing.

Caught Looking
**What goes through your mind when you catch a man checking you
out?**   —JOE, FT. LAUDERDALE, FLORIDA

It depends on who he is. If it's someone I'm attracted to, I'm thrilled
(as long as his look is subtle—if a guy leers, I assume he's a creep). If
it's a business associate, I feel belittled and insulted. If it's a guy sitting on the subway who looks like he might break his neck trying to
get a peek up my skirt, I feel threatened. As for construction workers,
dirty old men, and other stereotypical girl-watchers, any woman
knows it doesn't take much to get their attention. The click of high
heels alone can be enough to swing a whole row of hard hats our way.

For more honest answers about women, look for Ask the Men's Health Girl Next Door *wherever books are sold.*

3

THE HUNTING GROUND

Men love to hunt and fish. Nothing thrills us more than venturing into the wild and returning with an impressive quarry. If that quarry is a 5-foot-9 Rhodes scholar with legs that could shame a gazelle, so much the better.

But if a sharp pickup line were all you needed to hook the woman of your dreams, most guys would have hung up their hunting boots long ago. It takes good equipment and even better field sense to net a girl you won't want to throw back tomorrow.

We've talked to a lot of hunters (more than a few of them women) and learned what works in the field. Keep reading and get some game.

What's She Lookin' At?

Your belly, of course. But that's not all BY LISA JONES

1. Your well-muscled left forearm. Conveniently located directly above the very first thing I notice: your ring finger.

2. Your skin tone. 1 percent increase in tan = 47 percent increase in muscle tone.

3. Your resemblance to a rock. The Rock, Kid Rock, and all the rocks in between are equally attractive. So stop worrying about your body type. I like them all.

4. Your lungs. When you suck in your gut to impress me, I'm charmed silly.

5. Your stride. I love watching a man who's confident and in shape enough to run shirtless on the beach. You're barefoot, too? My heart is racing.

6. Your swim trunks. No Speedos, please. Just something stylish that shows off your moneymaker.

7. Your moneymaker. It's not what you're thinking. . . . I mean those lines that start near your hips and plummet down to your groin. They make you extremely hot . . . and me very, very bothered.

8. Your resemblance to Spider-Man. Women think Tobey Maguire is sexy. And you look like you can totally kick his ass.

9. Your calves. Especially when you're playing volleyball, sprinting for the Frisbee, riding your bike, or on your hands and knees helping a 5-year-old dig a sandcastle moat.

10. Your body in jeans, a linen dress shirt with rolled-up sleeves, and a backward baseball cap, all while you're splashing around with your black Lab in the surf at sunset. No, you're not wearing or doing that now. But I'm imagining you are, and you look freaking fetching.

11. Your rear view. Three words: lower-back dimples.

12. Your activity level. Have you been lying out? Or working out?

13. Your shoulder muscles. At some point I will determine whether or not you're strong enough to save me when I pretend to be caught in the undertow.

14. Your brainpan. Turn the right kind of pages and you can really turn me on. What are you reading—Melville? Or *Maxim* magazine?

15. Your accessories. Sunglasses and thong flip-flops = instant appeal.

16. Your attire. Salty, sandy, sun-kissed, and wearing a well-worn white T-shirt? I don't care what's under your shirt, because I can only think about getting naked.

17. Your courage. You didn't dip your toe to test the water before jumping in.

18. Your eyes. My eyes are open under these Jackie O. sunglasses, boy, and I can see you checking me out.

19. Your beer belly. A small one's not so bad. A tiny bit of soft flesh over the waistband is forgivable. (Just don't look like you swallowed the keg.)

20. Your belly button. Innie? Outie? Doesn't matter. Weirdly erotic, either way.

Pickup Tricks

How to go from zero to sexy in no time flat

BY KRISTINA GRISH

SELF-CONFIDENCE IS EXTREMELY SEXY to a woman. In fact, I'd go so far as to say that more than a man's good looks and more than his gentlemanly manner, confidence is the trigger trait that makes a woman want to get naked.

You remember that scene in *Goodfellas* when Ray Liotta takes Lorraine Bracco to the Copa? He slips her through the back door, tipping heavies the whole way, chatting up other wise guys, and finally ending up at a table in front of the stage. Liotta had something much more important than a roll of Franklins: He had confidence. And its effect on Bracco was clear. You knew he was getting laid that night.

"Women want a man with steel balls," says R. Don Steele, without a hint of irony in his voice. Steele is the author of *Body Language Secrets: A Guide during Courtship and Dating.* "This desire is evolutionary. Females want someone who's not going to run from a fight, a man who is confident in his ability to provide and protect."

Simply put, confidence gets the girl. So if you want to be more attractive to women, show your bravado. But I don't mean by pounding your chest or the drunk at the end of the bar. You don't have to be a wise guy to make yourself instantly irresistible. Here are some more-effective techniques.

WALK THIS WAY

"Women look first at your attire and second at how you walk," says Steele. Keep your wardrobe stylish and impeccable. Ashley Rothschild, a Los Angeles–based image consultant, suggests you emulate the look of a successful public man in your business arena. She also thinks you'd look hot in a leather jacket. It's classic. It's Steve McQueen. Your stride? Slow down. "Confident people are not in a hurry," says Steele. "But there's a difference between meandering and walking slowly with purpose. Always walk as if you know what you're doing and where you're going."

LOOK HER IN THE EYES

Tell her you love her dimples while gazing at her feet and you'll reek of emotional insecurity. If locking eyes with a stranger feels uncomfortable, focus on her mouth and she'll never know the difference, says Renee Piane, a motivational speaker and author of *Love Mechanics: Power Tools to Build Successful Relationships*. Staring elsewhere

The Overconfident Man

Too much bravado will leave you solo. Consider these nauseous nuances of the man who thinks too highly of himself.

- Brags about past conquests in front of my girlfriends.
- Waits until the last minute to ask me out, assuming I don't have plans.
- Is convinced he knows more about my anatomy/job/family than I do.
- Never admits I've won the argument.
- Always lets me win at pool.
- Wears sweatpants on a date.
- Calls the waitress "honey."
- Calls me "babe" on our first date.

Instant Confidence

There she is, sitting at the end of the bar, looking hot, looking so out of your league. You approach her praying she won't blow you off.

Instant rejection, predicts Jama Clark, Ph.D., author of *What the Hell Do Women Really Want?*. "If you're worried about what she'll think of you, you won't appear confident," Clark says. "Confident people tend to think, 'Will I like them?'"

This psychology can be applied to any social or business occasion. The next time you meet someone new, think to yourself, "I wonder if I'm going to like this person." Changing your mindset will transform your body language and speech from timid and self-conscious to friendly and self-assured.

makes you appear uninterested, inattentive, or insincere—especially during sweet talk. Also, she'll respond best to realistic compliments. "You're the physical embodiment of everything I look for in a woman" will immediately set off her bullsh-t alarm. "You've got beautiful eyelashes" will make her blush.

TAKE A COMPLIMENT

When she says she likes your dimples, simply "smile and say thank you," says Susan RoAne, author of *How to Work a Room*. Insecure people deflect compliments by asking, "Really? You think so?" or by listing reasons they don't deserve the compliment. Secure people accept praise gracefully and without ado.

CALL BEFORE DAY 3

She gave you her number. Use it within 48 hours or you'll look either scared or stupid for resorting to high-school mind games. Nervous? Manage the cold call as you would a business call. "Executives are action-oriented, gathering information and wasting no time in getting a project started. Apply these tactics to your private life," suggests Judith Coche, Ph.D., a clinical psychologist and professor at the University of Pennsylvania. "If you fail, move on. It's not about personal rejection—it's the business of making stuff work," says Coche.

PERFORM AT THE BEEP

If you get her voice mail, leave a message. To convey confidence, your voice should be deep and moderately loud. Stand up and hum a little before you call—it will bring your voice to the ideal pitch. "Say who you are, where you met, and why you're calling," says Kent Sayre, author of *Unstoppable Confidence*. "Don't seek her approval. Instead, ask a question that presupposes her interest in you, like, 'How soon would you like to get together?' That way it's not a matter of yes or no." Leave your number and ask her to call you back. If she doesn't, call her again a couple of days later.

DON'T EXPOSE YOUR NEGATIVES

When talking about yourself, keep it positive. Stick to your best attributes and the interests you're most passionate about. "Give the press-release version of you," says Kate Wachs, Ph.D., a psychologist and author of *Relationships for Dummies*. "Tell her everything good about your life that you wouldn't mind seeing in 4-inch-high letters on the front page of the newspaper the next morning."

HAVE A SEAT

Knowledge breeds confidence. Do you know where to sit during a dinner date? Always position yourself at a 90-degree angle to her in-

HOT WIRED

Percentage of singles who use online dating services:

53

SOURCE: Match.com—American Demographics

stead of straight on, says Steele. If she sits at the end of the table, sit in the first seat to her left. Turn toward her from the waist, which will give her the opportunity to turn toward you. "Women don't like a full-frontal assault. It's intimidating," says Steele. "A confident man realizes he should give the woman the choice to turn to him, and he is sure that she will."

INSTANT SEXPERT

The Touch Test

MH reader says: "Not sure if she's interested? If you've made it to a second round of drinks, initiate contact by touching her arm several times during the next 15 min-utes. Then abruptly stop all physical contact. If she's at-tracted to you, she'll fire a few strokes your way as soon as she realizes you've stopped touching her."
Sex scientist says: "Touch is a very important part of courtship. If she touches you back, it's a good sign. And you've moved up a notch in the courtship ritual."
SOURCE: *Helen Fisher, Ph.D., of Rutgers University, New Jersey, and author of* The First Sex

---

BE DIRECT

If you'd like to go into her apart-ment, tell her at the door—and skip the excuse about needing to use her bathroom. Want to kiss her goodnight? Go for it. "Kissing someone is an emotional thing, and asking [permission] diverts it into a cognitive realm instead," says Wachs. "Women hate that."

CELEBRATE HER SUCCESS

A confident man doesn't feel emasculated if the woman he's with makes more money than he does; he takes it as a compliment. "More than ever, successful single women earning more than $60K a year are looking for warm, loving men," says Coche. "They're more se-lective in their partner choice because they can afford to reprioritize." Truth is, she wouldn't be dating you if she didn't at least want to think you're a catch. It's when you believe it yourself that she'll be convinced.

Just Be a Man

Six simple suggestions—really simple

BY AMY SOHN

WHAT I WANT IN A MAN IS A MAN. After 10 years of dating scrubs, pushovers, and narcissistic artists, I recently fell in love with a guy named Jake. When I tried to figure out how Jake was different from the others, I realized it all came down to one thing: He's a man. And a man is not the same as a boy. Not even close.

Jake showers before coming over, listens to me when I talk, and doesn't have a conniption when he tries to say, "I love you." We don't have huge screaming arguments over his ability to commit. Instead, we eat candlelit dinners, argue about movies, and make stupid fart jokes.

If you, like most men, want to be a man but suspect that you're a hybrid, a Boy with Man Rising, here are a few basic steps to help with the transition. Think of them as an automatic bar mitzvah.

A MAN GOES DOWN

No excuses. No hesitation. Don't wait to be asked; offer. Don't do it for 2 minutes and then resurface happily, expecting some sort of trophy for participation. Stoop to conquer and you will. Don't complain about hair, smell, consistency. If there's a problem down there, you're allowed to have second thoughts about the girl, but in general, keep your mouth shut.

Be willing to stay there about as long as your favorite sitcom lasts, and possibly longer. If she taps your shoulder and says, "It's okay, you can come up," respond with, "Is there anything I could be doing better?" because she doesn't really mean, "It's okay, you can come up." She means, "You need to move to the left," or, "Try the Japanese alphabet, not the English." Half the tappers out there just don't believe you want to be down under, so the best way to convince them you're for real is to refuse the tap. It may take some discipline, but remember: You will be rewarded.

A MAN KNOWS HE IS NOT THE ONLY MEMBER OF THE RELATIONSHIP WHO HAS A CAREER

As "nesty" as women may be, when we enter relationships, we can feel conflicted, too. We worry that we're not spending enough time with our friends, our work, our family, and, believe it or not, ourselves. So when a man goes on and on about his job and how demanding it is, he comes off as a self-centered jerk, unless he's Ari Fleischer. So the next time you hear yourself saying, "I really need to focus on my work right now," to explain where you're coming from or to get out of the relationship, do the girl a favor and dump her so she can find somebody else.

A MAN IS CURIOUS

Women are trained to ask questions and listen. That's what we do with our girlfriends. It doesn't mean we always want to be listening to you the whole time, though. I once dated a guy who went on about his job for the entire length of a 5-hour car ride, without ever asking me about what I do, which is write a column about sex—not exactly a conversation stopper. That was our last date.

SEE SPOT SAY, "SEE YA"

Percentage of Americans who wouldn't consider dating someone who didn't like their pet:

90

A MAN FEELS

I once had a man tell me, a few months into our relationship, that he felt as if I'd been pushing him away. I immediately burst into tears—not out of guilt, but from gratitude. The fact that he could voice such a complaint was proof to me not only that he cared, but that he cared enough to communicate.

A little goes a long way. So many men have a hard time expressing their feelings about anything, from the taste of their blackened salmon to the reason they cried at *Frequency*, that we're overjoyed just to hear them say something as simple as "I feel close to you right now."

A MAN BENDS

Maybe because like attracts like, I've dated more than my share of stick-in-the-muds—and paid the price. I once told a boyfriend I felt he had been patronizing me in public, and he said, "I wasn't! I have a novelist's eye for detail, and I can tell you I wasn't!" What made me mad wasn't that he disagreed with my interpretation, but that he seemed to think I was objectively, qualitatively incorrect. People are never incorrect when they say what they feel.

When you find yourself in one of those fights where, as Bob Dylan put it, "everything I'm saying, you can say it just as good," try to bend a little. Tell her you can see how she might feel a certain way, even if you didn't intend for her to. Women appreciate it when you give them the benefit of the doubt.

That's it. Take these reminders out into the bars and restaurants and streets, and women will be putty in your manly hands. But before you do, destroy this so your future girlfriend doesn't find it, because the most important rule of manhood is . . .

A MAN MAKES MANHOOD LOOK EASY

Her Clothing Arguments

6 smart, sexy women with something to say
about the clothes on your back

BY BRIAN BOYÉ

RULE #1: DON'T FALL FOR FASHION TRENDS

After 17 years as a supermodel, Naomi Campbell has formulated a
few opinions about style . . . and she likes men who have a few opinions of their own. To impress this famously fickle style maven, "don't
try to be perfect," she warns. Have the confidence to mix things up—
like marrying a top-of-the-line blazer with jeans—"and don't try to
look like a shop window." Despite being linked to some of the world's
coolest designers, such as close friends Domenico Dolce and Stefano
Gabbana, she likes a man who knows how to pick out his own outfits. Just one caveat: Don't wear anything shiny or glitzy. "Leave that
for me."

One more thing: You'll have to make your style decisions fast if
you want to keep up with Campbell. Last fall, she added "business
owner" to her résumé, when she launched her own marketing and
event-planning firm, NC.Connect, whose clients include Dolce &
Gabbana. With multiple cell phones engaged at all times and a
schedule that would leave mere mortals breathless, can this multi-
tasker handle more work? "Why not?" she laughs. "I was doing all of
this for free already."

NAOMI'S NO-NO'S:
- Be a man, not a mannequin.
- No Western belts.
- No tight pants.
- No big-heeled shoes.
- Oh, and skip the skivvies. "I don't like men in underwear,"
she declares.

RULE #2: BE SOFT TO THE TOUCH

Gail O'Grady was raised in the Midwest and now lives in Los Angeles, but she has always identified with the South. The star of the NBC series *American Dreams* says that a little of that Southern gentility and charm can make men irresistible to women. When it comes to clothes, O'Grady likes hers sexy and his neat, clean, and classic. The voluptuous actress, who made her mark in television on *NYPD Blue*, likes a man in natural fibers, such as cotton and summer-weight wool, and loves a crisp white dress shirt. Whether it's worn with rolled-up sleeves and a pair of jeans or buttoned up with a pinstriped suit, "there's nothing sexier," she says.

GAIL'S GUIDELINES:

• Don't pull your pants up too high—dress pants, she says, should button an inch or more below your navel.

• Do wear natural fibers in the spring and summer—avoid nylon and polyester. "Buy clothes that feel soft in your hands, because they'll feel soft in hers," O'Grady says.

• Do wear a dress shirt with the sleeves rolled up. "I love a man who takes off his tie and rolls up his sleeves," she says.

RULE #3: LOOSEN UP!

She's tight with Hollywood's A-list. She's traveled the world, reporting on drugs in Colombia, wars in Afghanistan, and nuclear weapons in Russia. She's a marathon runner and former colleague of Barbara Walters on *The View*. Serious stuff. But when it comes to men, Lisa Ling is interested in casual dudes with cool sneakers and baggy jeans. Go figure.

It's the not-pulled-together look that attracts Ling, the host of MSNBC's *National Geographic Ultimate Explorer*. "I like guys who are dressed informally," she says, ticking off the requirements: Jeans—slightly baggy. Sneakers—vintage. Shirts—untucked. "Shiny, tight shirts?" She grimaces. "No can do."

LISA'S LIST:

• Don't try to dress up casual clothes by tucking them in tightly; leave T-shirts and sweaters loose.

• Do wear your jeans low and roomy—just above the hips is about right.

• Do wear cool accessories. "Watches and shoes are things that men can be playful with," Ling says.

RULE #4: GO LONG, STAY LOW

"Longer is definitely better," says singer/songwriter Dana Glover. This she is sure of. She likes men in long jeans, preferably "bunched up at the bottom." Short, high-waisted jeans are a real turnoff, says this flame-haired, piano-playing beauty. Denim has come up frequently for her lately. In the whirlwind of publicity for her debut CD, titled *Testimony* (Dreamworks Records), Glover has been photographed often—usually in her favorite pair of blue jeans. "I'm a one-jean woman," she says in her slow, intoxicating drawl. But she likes all kinds of jeans on men. Although she's currently married only to her music, there's no doubt that increased visibility will bring about changes soon. Follow these tips to catch Glover's eye:

DANA'S DO'S AND DON'TS:

• Do master the art of dressing casually. "Casual and confident is cool," she says.

• Do wear low-rise jeans, and don't worry if they're a little too long.

• Don't look as if you tried too hard.

• "Designer labels are good but not necessary," she says. Men who appreciate good fabric and great style get bonus points.

RULE #5: BE FUNCTIONAL BUT FUNKY

She's tall, blonde, and beautiful, but 6'3" athlete, author, and model Gabrielle Reece backs up her looks with performance. And that's what she wants her man to do—well, with his clothes, at least. Whether you're on the golf course or the volleyball court, she wants to see that your athletic wear is about function, not fashion. But that doesn't mean you can't show a little bit of pizzazz. "I dress in what's right for me, and that's how I like to see guys dress. When I see a guy who's funky but can pull it all together," she adds, "that shows me he has flair and imagination."

You'll need it to keep up with Reece. While serving as a spokeswoman for Lean Results (learn more at leanresultsdiet.com), she's spent the past 2 years in intensive training for a new career as a professional golfer. Reece will compete in her first pro-am tournament at the end of May. "My goal is to get my ass kicked on the satellite tours and build up enough experience to qualify for the LPGA." In the meantime, here are her goals for you.

GABBY'S GIFTS OF GARB:

• Don't wear too many labels.

• Don't wear loafers. "They trip me out," she says.

• Do wear sport-appropriate fitness apparel—and make sure you can move in it.

INSTANT SEXPERT

Love at First Site

A personal reference beats a great resumé every time, in job hunting and especially in dating. Among single women, nothing beats a recommendation from another woman. A popular dating site called greatboyfriends.com puts that power to work for you.

Here's how: You ask a friendly ex or a gal pal to post your profile and vouch for you (and maybe to explain the scars and arrest record). Then interested women read all about you and deluge you with passionate e-mails—or at least send a few cautious, exploratory ones. (Often they'll first contact the woman who recommended you.)

Cocreator E. Jean Carroll suggests that you choose your wittiest female friend to write your post. Use a picture of you with your dog or with nieces and nephews; these tend to get more responses. And tell your friend to leave out anything about That Weekend—raunchy sexual references are forbidden.

- Do exercise. "Fit guys look better in clothes," she says.
- Do trade in the sports gear for a pair of old jeans when the game is over.

RULE #6: SHOW OFF YOUR PHYSIQUE

Catherine Dent spends plenty of time around tough guys in her role as Officer Danny Sofer on the Golden Globe–winning show *The Shield*. So it's no wonder she's gained an affinity for the uniforms of men who are always ready for action—and who wear clothes that show it. "Good health is sexier than any label," says the Louisiana native. With the right pair of shoes, a simple pair of Levi's and a Gap T-shirt are enough to turn a woman on, she says—"although a man in a really good-looking, well-cut suit is pretty hot, too." The key is vitality: If you take care of yourself physically, don't hide it under baggy sweaters and pleated pants.

And Dent's been around enough sharp guys to know whereof she speaks: She appeared with Jim Carrey in *The Majestic* and Greg Kinnear in *Auto Focus*. As she puts it, "I love playing with the boys." Fine by us.

CATHERINE'S CAVEATS:

- Don't let your wife or girlfriend dress you.
- Don't overdo the cologne. "You shouldn't have to cover up who you are."
- Do wear well-fitted business clothes—shirts, suits, and flat-front pants—if you've got the body for them.
- Do get a shoe shine before you arrive.
- Do keep jewelry to a minimum. "I want a guy to be a guy," she says.

"You're Going to Wear That?"

Pleated khakis, leather "mandals," and other style choices
that will kill your sex life dead

BY LAUREN WEISBERGER

THE SCENE: A SMALL GROUP OF WOMEN sharing apple martinis
at a trendy bar; one is being grilled on her first date with a new guy.

"So, give us the details—what's he like?"

The obviously smitten woman sighs. "Well," she says, "incredibly
funny. Super-smart. Great dresser." The others nod approvingly, each
picturing a suave, sophisticated man who can make her laugh, make her
think, and look good while doing it. If you want to be successful with
women, gentlemen, this is your goal. And since I don't have a bagful of
tricks to make you smarter or funnier, let's jump right to the clothes.

If you acknowledge that you're style challenged, your primary
focus should be moving away from the blue-dress-shirt/pleated-khaki-
pants nightmare. Start slowly, but be persistent: Keep the blue shirt
but buy a pair of plain-front black pants, making sure they're long
enough to touch the ground when you're not wearing shoes. Repeat
this mantra while shopping and you won't go wrong: Tapered Ankles
Are Style Death. If you're unsure of what tapered ankles are, chances
are you're wearing them: The width of the legs should not be notice-
ably narrower at the ankle than at the knee. Memorize this.

Once you feel comfortable in your new pants, try topping them
with a different-color shirt or a fitted cashmere sweater, and add a pair
of squarish-toed black shoes sans laces (if you're under 35), or some
simple, nonshiny loafers (if you're 35 or older).

For those of you who've already graduated from the classic frat-boy uniform, congratulations are in order. But you're not off the hook—yet. Your focus should be on achieving that ever-elusive "just gay enough" look: Done right, it sends women the message that you're sensitive and cultured and stylish. Some understated risk-taking is your best bet. Break from the more obvious solid-shirt/patterned-tie look by pairing a tiny-dotted tie with a boldly striped shirt. Embrace colors—cornflower blue, lemon yellow, burnt orange—and incorporate them into your outfits without going overboard. Nothing's hotter than a straight guy who's self-assured enough to wear a pink shirt or sport some bright, funky socks.

Regardless of where you fall on the fashion-forward to fashion-forewarned spectrum, there are some general rules that should save you from utter humiliation. Light gray suits, no matter how nice, look cheap on almost everybody—a charcoal gray or classic black works much better. And avoid at all costs anything from those giant menswear supermarkets. Jeans are an integral part of every man's wardrobe, and it's best to keep them pure: Buy them in as long a length as you can stand, aim for some bootleg but no bell-bottom, wear them low on the hips, and avoid any little "extras," including, but not limited to, buckles, leather, holes, and excessive prefading. Find these jeans and never take them off, especially if you pair them with a fitted white T-shirt and black shoes, or cool, retro-style sneakers like Pumas in any color except white.

If you feel too old for hipster kicks, follow your instincts: You can't go wrong with a pair of the classic gray New Balances. And while we're talking about shoes, resist the temptation to think you're the one who can pull off those brown leather sandals (a.k.a. "mandals"); a pair of Adidas sports sandals or just the classic Reef flip-flops are infinitely preferable.

And, if all else fails, fake it. Suck in (or eliminate) your gut, plaster a smile on your face, and approach her as if you just stepped off the Armani runway. Confidence is still the sexiest outfit of all.

A Simple Plan

A Conversation with John Fate

I s it possible for an ordinary, average-looking guy to date beautiful women? Two ordinary, average-looking guys say, emphatically, "Yes."

Four years ago, after a typical New Year's Eve—no dates, no sex, and no prospects for either—John Fate and Steve Reil resolved to spend as much time as it took to discover the secret to making women want them. Today, the Virginia twentysomethings, neither of whom have any formal training as dating and sex coaches, make a convincing case for having cracked the code. In their self-published book, *Make Every Girl Want You*, and at classes they teach at the Learning Annex in New York City and San Francisco, they give men a program that, they say, can turn luckless losers into ladies men.

Anchoring their method are three key behaviors: compassion, compliments, and reassurance, or CCR, as Fate and Reil call it. If a guy is patient—forging friendships with women instead of hitting on them, for example, and waiting for women to make the first move—and if he practices CCR daily, beautiful women will be attracted to him, regardless of his superficial qualities.

We talked to John Fate about the program.

What makes you and Steve Reil qualified to give sex and relationship advice?

Where we've come from and where we've gotten to. We used to be absolutely pathetic. In college, girls wouldn't be friends with us, they wouldn't date us. Girls wouldn't go out with us, girls wouldn't hook up with us, nothing. It was only after those years of pathetic-ness that we really set out to become friends with women and understand what they look for in guys.

Now we can get women, and a lot of guys say, "These guys know what it's like to be pathetic, and they figured out how to change."

You and Steve basically said to each other, "Let's figure out women this year." Was it really that easy?

Hell, no. It took 6 months before one of us even got laid once. We'd work at our regular jobs during the day, 40 or 50 hours a week, and then we'd come home and do this. A lot of it was simply going out with women and spending time with women. We'd talk on the phone nonstop and compare notes.

How did things finally turn around?

We had a few hypotheses. One of them was, "Let's set out and really try to become friends with girls. Let's not try to sleep with them, let's not try to date them, and maybe if we build up a network of female friends, (a) we'll start to understand women better and learn more about them or (b) maybe we'll meet a lot more women because women know other women.

We made a list of even our most remote acquaintances, girls we knew from UVA, girls who worked with him, girls who worked with me, anywhere we could go to meet and make friends with more women. It reached the point where we had so many female friends that women would be calling us to do this or that. In 3 months, we went from having no female friends to having women calling us constantly. We were running all over the place.

At what point did you decide you'd write a book?
I guess a few months in we started kidding around about it. Once we started to see the results of our methods, we were like, "Whoa, we're really on to something. A few months ago, we were like any other guys, and now women love us." Maybe after a year or so we decided to write the book.

Let's look at your dating strategy itself. You realized early on that meeting random women may not be the most efficient way for guys to become acquainted with and date women. What did you learn about dating that took you by surprise?
The actual way to communicate with and treat women. What most guys do is talk nonstop about themselves. They try to impress the woman overtly. One of the first things we realized is that women like men so much better when we sit and listen to them talk about themselves. That was completely counterintuitive to anything we'd ever done.

Another thing that surprised us was how smart it was to be friends with girls who already had boyfriends. When meeting a girl with a boyfriend, typically most guys try to get out of that conversation in 30 seconds. But these girls are the best kind to have around, especially if the boyfriend is out of town. It's not because you want them to cheat on their boyfriends. These girls are lonely. These girls are looking for fun people to hang out with and fun things to do. They serve as a great vouch for you. Invite her along to anything and other girls will be so intrigued that you have this beautiful, platonic friend by your side.

One of the three cornerstones of the CCR program is giving girls lots of compliments. Why?

Giving a girl a compliment is so much easier than trying to impress her. Women want to feel comfortable and nonthreatened. They want emotional support, and compliments are the easiest way to give it.

Also, complimenting a girl is a really easy way to get her to talk and start conversation without grasping for topics. If you compliment her necklace and she tells you she got it in Italy with her family, she's giving you a couple different angles to keep the conversation going. You could ask about her family; you could ask about Italy. It's amazing.

Doesn't complimenting people all the time sound insincere? Did women get suspicious when you started being more complimentary?

No, we were able to do it rather flawlessly. We made the change 100 percent, and that's important. Even hanging out with the guys, we were complimentary and respectful. Am I saying you can't make crass, rude comments sometimes? No. But things do get back to people. You'll be hanging out with a mixed group of guys and girls and one guy will repeat a comment that was originally said when it was just guys around. That can get you in trouble.

Also, the new personality was overall a more enjoyable personality for everyone. It was noticeable to our close friends, but not in a bad manner. No one said, "You guys have become so fake." I think the word we heard most was "mature." People said, "I really enjoy being around you much more."

When you compliment women, what do you usually say?

Women accessorize, so it's easy to find something. When they go out, they put on all sorts of stuff. They put on scarves, jackets, necklaces, even glitter. Everything is a potential compliment. Once you are aware of what you can compliment women on, you never need to fish for compliments. I can look at a woman now and easily pick out something about her to compliment.

In your book, you point to eye color as one of the best compliments features to compliment. Aren't women used to being complimented on their eyes? We'd think they wouldn't be that impressed by it.

It's not so much complimenting a girl's eye color as it is remembering her eye color and complimenting her on it later. That's a powerful compliment. Women know the eye color of every single guy. Some women can name the eye color of every hot guy in Hollywood. It's like guys with breast size. Every guy has in his memory the breast size of the women they know. They even remember the clothing that makes girl's breasts look good. If they are sitting around talking, they'll be like "Jennifer . . . she's got okay breasts, but they really look great when she wears that low-dipping red tank top.

But so few guys know eye color. I make it a point to notice eye color and try to remember it. It's amazing when you are on the phone and a girl says, "I'm surprised you remembered me from the party," and you say, "Yeah, you have great blue eyes."

The second part of CCR is compassion. What, exactly, do you mean by compassion, and why is it important?

All three parts of CCR are important, but compassion is a notch above the other two because it really conveys that you are interested in the woman as a person. What we tell guys is, "If you are talking to a woman, ask her questions and convey that you are interested in what she has to say." Most guys talk about themselves and treat women as sex objects. When a woman meets a man who treats her like a person, she is intrigued.

Compassion is really the one part of this program that will encourage a girl to open up to you and make her feel like you are inter-

ested in who she is. You can compliment a girl all day long, but if you
don't make eye contact and show you are actually interested, you are
not going to get anywhere.

It's probably toughest for guys to do this part, because we are not
used to the passive stuff. We're taught that if someone has a problem,
help them solve it. When women have a problem, what they really want
is someone to listen to them. We found out from female friends that
women don't want solutions. Women are like, "When you try to give me
a solution, I feel like you don't want to listen. I feel like you're saying
'Here's what you should do. Now shut up.'" Women want people to sit
and listen for 10 to 15 minutes so they can get it out of their systems.

How is the final part of CCR, reassurance, different from compassion?
What most guys don't realize is that women simply need reassurance.
When guys have had a bad day, all we want to do is get drunk. If we've
lost our job, we don't need someone to tell us, "Oh, don't worry. You'll
find another job." We know that we will; in the meantime, however,
we need to get drunk—that's how we cope!

With women, on the other hand, reassurance goes a long way. If
a woman has had a bad day at work, for example, you can tell her,
"Hey, I know things haven't been going well at work, but things will
turn around soon. I know how smart you are, and you're a very hard
worker, and your boss will start to recognize that, and things will get
better." That simple statement can make a woman's day. I've seen it
improve a woman's mood tremendously in just a matter of minutes.

**You suggest the one thing that guys don't want to read in a dating book:
Relinquish desire and don't press the issue of kissing, sex, et cetera. Why
will guys get more if they try less?**
It's the most amazing thing. Most guys, when they approach a woman,
give her the wrong impression. Most guys, even though they don't
mean to, just send the signals that all they want to do is sleep with a

woman. As we've learned from our many female friends, that's such a turn-off! What we've learned to do is, the night we first meet a woman, not to try to sleep with her, not to try to take her home, not to ask her out on the spot. Just have a great conversation and get her contact info. We've found that when we try to take a woman home the night we've met her, we fail *way* more than we succeed. When, however, we have the patience to simply get her contact info the night that we've met her, a woman is very willing to give us her contact info and very willing to go out with us the following week. All because we didn't make the mistake of treating her like a sex object up-front.

Do you really believe your book's title? Can any guy have any girl?
No, but his chances are a lot better. We say 10 percent of guys are really good-looking. Another 10 percent are really ugly. The final 80 percent are just normal guys. That's our audience. Really attractive women are willing to give these guys chances if they act the right way. It's not like with women, where guys look at them and say, "Oh, she's pretty cute; she's hot; she's kind of cute." Guys can put women in a million categories. With women, it's 10 percent on the top, 10 percent on the bottom, and the other 80 percent have to differentiate themselves through behavior.

There are exceptions. If you've known a girl for a long time, chances are she's not going to be romantically interested in you right away. But in the book, we talk about second- and third-generational friends. These are the girls who we were introduced to by the girls we already knew. And these friends of friends just loved us to no end because we had the original girls to vouch for us.

So it's not really "Make Every Girl Want You." It's more like "Make a Lot More Girls Want You."
Yeah, or "Make Every Type of Girl Want You." The biggest problem we see when we teach our seminars at the Learning Annex is when

guys want a specific type of girl and pester us, "Hey I'm really into Asian women. Can you give me tips?" I say, "This is what usually works for women in American society and American culture." Or we have guys who are hung up on one specific girl. Usually, by the time they come to CCR, they've already screwed up and it's unrecoverable. We tell guys, "Go out, meet other women. You'll forget about her in no time."

How well would you say you do, percentage-wise?
The number one most hated question we get is, "So are you so good you can walk up to any girl and pick her up?" Jeez. Hell, no. The difference is, I'm smart enough to know not to walk up to random girls on the street and try to pick them up. We say, "Don't go up to random women." You can definitely do it, but if you want to have a high success rate and maintain your confidence and dignity, that's not what this is about.

I can get accurate contact info from girls I approach about 50 percent of the time. That's a big change for me.

QUICKIES

A Clue That She's on the Pill

If you're a certain type of man, there's a certain kind of woman who's looking for you. In a series of trials, Scottish researchers found that women taking birth-control pills have different tastes in men than women who aren't on the Pill. The studies suggested that women on birth-control pills were more attracted to men with rugged, manly features, such as strong, wide jaws and big cheekbones, while women not taking the Pill preferred men with softer, more feminine features. The reason appears to be a shift in hormone levels caused by the Pill, say the researchers.

Work the Flattery

When you approach a woman's body, exercise your tongue to its fullest potential—conversationally, that is. Your goal: Caress her sensitive spots without appearing opportunistic.

Hair

Keep it general, like how it shines. No style tips: "She'll blame you if it doesn't work," says Michael Cunningham, Ph.D., a psychologist and professor of communications at the University of Louisville.

Breasts

Avoid the potentially offensive terms: hooters, knockers, udders. Create your own vocabulary. "Women fall in love with what they hear," says Ann Convery, a presentation coach who specializes in male-female communication.

Lips Talk

Is it their size, shape, or color that turns you on? Point out specific features that are unique to her, says Paul Joannides, author of *Guide to Getting It On*.

Butt

"Use jargon like 'tush' or 'booty.' 'Ass' is sexy. But 'behind,' 'backside,' and 'rear' sound old-fashioned," Convery says. "Convince her you love it: Adore it, claim it, name it, pay attention to it."

Belly

Discuss her softer angles and curves when she's on her back, so her belly is flat. "Tell her, 'I love how you look when . . . ,'" suggests Convery. "This makes her an active participant in seduction, not just a passive recipient of flattery."

Legs

"Say they're in good shape. You'll lose some credibility if you say you love them and she doesn't," says Cunningham.

LOST IN THE CONDOM AISLE

Condoms are like Heinz ketchup—there are 57 varieties. There are latex, ribbed, spermicidal. What does it all mean?

Considering that your hot dog might be coming in contact with HIV, gonorrhea, chlamydia, syphilis, or genital herpes, and that it could cause unwanted pregnancies, you're smart to ask. Although no condom is 100 percent guaranteed (accidents will happen), they're still the best form of protection. Here are a few condom pros and cons, thanks to the experts at the Mayo Clinic.

Latex

These provide highly effective barriers against pregnancy and STDs and are the most reliable preventive measure against the transmission of HIV.

Plastic

Proven in recent, limited lab studies to be an effective barrier against HIV, but unlike latex condoms, they're prone to slipping off.

Animal Skin (Lambskin)

They can stop sperm, but viruses and bacteria pass "Go."

Female Condoms

The plus side: they're her problem, not yours. Minus side: They feel like having sex with a plastic bag.

Novelty Condoms

Avoid them. You are not a "novelty," and these condoms rarely protect against STDs.

"More Sensitive"

Synonym for thinner, with an increased risk of tearing.

"Stronger"

Synonym for thicker, meaning there's less breakthrough risk—and less sensation.

Size

In condoms, it counts, so be honest. If it's too tight, it's likely to break. If you buy XXL and you're not, the slippage factor is huge.

INSTANT SEXPERT

Which Way's Up?

Are condoms complicated? Evidently they are for men on the campus of Indiana University. A survey identified these problems.

Bad timing. Some 43 percent had begun intercourse, then stopped to put on a condom.

Tutorial: Too late, Hoosiers. That's like hollering for defensive help after your man has driven the lane for a layup. Put it on first. It says so right on the box.

Upside down. Thirty percent had started putting it on backward, then flipped it over and continued. So any semen from the tip of the penis had a front-row fun ride into the Tunnel of Love and Unwanted Pregnancy.

Tutorial: Start unrolling it on a finger first. If you put it on wrong, toss it out and grab another.

No space at the tip. Forty percent did this, and it can lead to breaking or leaking.

Tutorial: To leave some room, pinch the tip of the condom while unrolling it.

Ribbed

Same protection for you, a little more tickle for her.

Lubricated

May reduce the risk of tearing.

Spermicidal

These offer slightly more protection against pregnancy, thanks to the spermicide nonoxynol-9 (N-9), but they aren't HIV or STD killers, according to the Centers for Disease Control and Prevention.

SPRAY-ON SEX APPEAL

Axe deodorant body spray is a fragrance and deodorant that you spray under your arms and all over your body. You'll save 50 bucks on a new bottle of cologne—enough to replace the shirt you'll be losing: 62 percent of women have "stolen" a guy's shirt because they loved the way it smelled, according to a recent survey of 500 women. We like the Tsunami scent. $5 at drugstores.

COLOGNE CLASS

Cologne overload smells like desperation. But maybe you're reapplying because you put it on incorrectly in the first place. Here are some hints from Daniel Annese, a vice-president of marketing for Estée Lauder:

- Apply to hot spots such as the wrists and behind the ears. A little scent inside your elbows or behind your knees will waft upward.
- Deodorant soaps don't distinguish between body odor and good cologne; they'll wipe it all out. If your cologne fades, switch to a nondeodorant soap without triclosan.
- Look at a company's entire line to see if there are other products with the same scent. Layering will make your bouquet last all day.

Find a Keeper: The Best Places to Meet Women

You already know you won't find your true match in a bar; what would you tell the (future) kids? "Mom was bangin' Sake Bombers when we met, so I thought she was easy." Go places where you'll have more than booze (and desperation) in common with potential mates. Our picks:

Art Museums

About two-thirds of visitors to art museums are women. And they're usually educated professionals, says Cara Egan, public-relations manager for the Seattle Art Museum.

• Why: She'll assume you're somewhat intelligent. There's freedom of movement and speech. And it's flattering to talk to her about what she thinks of a painting. "If she agrees with you, it's a safe bet that she's interested," says Marian Dunn, Ph.D., a clinical associate professor of psychiatry at SUNY Downstate Medical Center. Egan says go with abstracts: "They're always open to interpretation."

• Insider opinion: Most big museums have evening events, which are perfect for mingling. "A conversation about art can end right there in the gallery or turn into a coffee date at the museum café," says Janet Asaro, director of public relations for the Anchorage Museum of History and Art.

NASCAR

Women make up 40 percent of NASCAR fans; the Daytona 500 race alone gets more than 150,000 spectators. Do the math: She's out there.

• Why: The noise of the race will excite her and raise her testosterone levels. "An increase in testosterone leads to an increase in the sex drive of both men and women," says Al Cooper, Ph.D., director of the San Jose Marital and Sexuality Center.

• Insider opinion: "The best-looking women are always down by the track—but they're usually dating the drivers," says Bill Janitz, public-relations manager for Michigan International Speedway. There are more women than available (i.e., unhospitalized) drivers, so your odds are good.

Soccer Games

Major League Soccer crowds are 47 percent women, so the girl-to-guy ratio is better than at other professional sporting events (excluding the WNBA, the LPGA, or any sport that has judges).

• Why: If she's watching MLS, she's not your average woman in a halter top in the bleachers at Wrigley. She's an enthusiast, a passionate believer, which makes for better conversation. If you can connect with her on that level . . . Goal!

• Insider opinion: "Women go to the games to see the soccer players, so it's a good opportunity for the men in the stands to see good-looking girls," says Jed Mettee, director of media relations for the San Jose Earthquakes.

DILBERT GETS LUCKY

It's a standard workplace warning: Don't dip your pen in the office inkwell; don't fish off the company pier; don't put your drill in the shop's toolbox. Okay, already—except that your chances of finding a compatible mate at work are a lot better than your shot at finding one at a bar. In a survey by Janet Lever, Ph.D., a sociologist at California State University at Los Angeles, 65 percent of men questioned had had at least one office romance. And 45 percent of those men reported that the romance worked out—lasting a year or longer. So ignore the warnings, but follow the rules:

Ask Out

Wait 3 months after starting a new job before asking a coworker for a date. When you're new, you're being judged. "If you start dating too soon, you'll be in the spotlight. Nobody needs that kind of pressure," says Julianne Balmain, author of *Office Kama Sutra*.

Do the Evening Check-In

Swing by her cube briefly on your way out the door. If it goes well, make it a habit. "It opens up the evening and makes it easy to go from 'I've had enough of those damn EPS reports' to 'Want to go grab a beer?'" Balmain says.

Go Out

Stay on your game. Keep your work top-notch when dating. "If people are jealous, worried, or angered by your relationship, don't give them any further cause to complain," says Dennis Powers, author of *The Office Romance: Playing with Fire without Getting Burned*.

Be Up Front

Everybody knows anyway, "even if you think you're being discreet," says Rosemary Agonito, Ph.D., author of *Dirty Little Secrets: Sex in the Workplace*. Don't make an announcement, but if someone asks, don't lie. Then make a joke about improving synergy.

Get Out

Time your breakup right. Always do it on a Friday, so she has the weekend to recover if she's upset. But stick around, and resist the urge to break up before you leave for vacation or a holiday. "By the time you come back, she could have total control of the breakup spin," Balmain says.

Take a Break

"Wait 30 days before hopping back in the saddle," Balmain says, or coworkers could see you as a serial romancer. And by then you'll know if your ex might try to sabotage the new liaison, so you can act accordingly.

How to Skirt a Date Disaster

Any shlub can act smooth when the date is going smoothly. A rough patch reveals the truly cool.

She's Wearing a Hot Red Dress. You're in Jeans.

Say, "Wow, you look beautiful," suggests Carolyn Bushong, a Denver psychotherapist. Offer to change clothes or to take her somewhere you'd both be comfortable. Show that you understand the situation.

The Restaurant Is Awful

Tell the waiter you're not happy, but don't become irate. She'll see a polite man with high standards. Then take her out for coffee or a drink someplace nice. Leave her with something tangible, like a flower. "The strong positive memory will override the bad experience at the restaurant," says Jeff St. John, Ph.D., a relationship expert in Beverly Hills.

You Run Into an Ex

Introduce the women by first names—no titles—and keep it short. If your date asks, tell her you dated ages ago, nothing more. "Being friendly with your ex will make a good impression," says John Eagan, a relationship author. "It shows that you're not a creep."

ASK THE GIRL
NEXT DOOR
The honest truth about women from our lovely neighbor

Insert or Delete?

If a woman flirts with me by e-mail, does that mean she wants me to ask her out? —ANONYMOUS

If she's single and your age, and you've met before and had a good time together, then yes. Trading e-mails is different from a telephone conversation—sexual innuendo and coy remarks don't just slip out; they're carefully crafted. I've had plenty of female friends send their barely flirtatious e-mail drafts to me to ask if I thought they sounded desperate. So if you get the impression that she's flirting, she probably is, and you should go ahead and ask her out if you're interested. One warning: Some women will freak out if a man starts to flirt too much by e-mail, especially if they've never met the guy. They get paranoid that they're dealing with a cyber pervert. So keep the sexy banter to a minimum. Better yet, be a gentleman: Pick up the phone and invite her out for coffee.

You Might O.D. on Mickey

The woman I'm interested in dating has a 6-year-old child. Anything I should be cautious about? —EDWARD L., PIERRE, SOUTH DAKOTA

Just don't kid yourself. If you're not ready to end a date at 10 P.M. because her babysitter has a curfew, spend Saturday mornings in the park instead of sleeping in, talk about things like health insurance and education over dinner, and kiss spontaneous weekend getaways goodbye—then don't do it. The life of a guy who seriously dates a single mom isn't much different from the life of a dad. Not that that's bad. In fact, there's a huge upside, too. Kids and their single moms can be incredibly fun. What other grown woman would be psyched to go to Six Flags on a Friday night? And it's just cool to have a relationship with a kid. Even getting casually involved in a child's life can actually make you happier and more fulfilled. You might even like it. Read Nick Hornby's *About a Boy* to see exactly what I mean.

No Half-Baked Idea

Just curious: What's the most romantic thing a guy has done for you? —BRAD D., SCRANTON, PENNSYLVANIA

My boyfriend once baked me a chocolate cake on my birthday, then presented me with two tickets to see Spinal Tap live at Carnegie Hall. Spinal Tap was hilarious, but the cake was definitely the most romantic thing because it took thought and effort, and it made me feel really wanted. After the show we went back to his apartment to finish it up. And we had some dessert, too.

Screen Games

What's your opinion of online dating? *Men's Health* magazine recently ran a feature about it, but it was by a man.
—RICH, BY (APPROPRIATELY) E-MAIL

I'm surprised to say this, but online dating has finally lost its losers-only reputation. At least a dozen attractive, cool, successful women I know have warmed up to the idea of searching for a beau online. Kara, a brainiac babe who uses personals on nerve.com, says she likes knowing from the get-go what kind of relationship a guy wants. When you meet someone at a bar, you can't come right out and ask, "So, is your ultimate goal to hook up, date casually, or get serious?" Yet online that's standard profile content. I also think that because we now regularly do so many intimate things online—banking, buying underwear, chatting with friends—finding a date that way doesn't seem so outlandish.

Damaged Goods

What do never-been-married women in their 20s think of divorced men? I'm 32 and dating again. —PERRY, FLAGSTAFF, ARIZONA

In the merciless words of my friend Mackenzie, "A recently divorced guy is a no-no. He's on the rebound times 1,000." The problem is, you're not going to want another serious relationship anytime soon, and we know it. So unless we're specifically looking for a casual fling, you might as well have been recently paroled. But after a year or two, the stigma will wear off and you'll have that experienced-older-man mystique going for you.

For more honest answers about women, look for Ask the Men's Health Girl Next Door *wherever books are sold.*

4

THE NEXT STEP

Eventually, any guy with half a brain realizes that the best part of dating is the last part, where you finally find someone to spend the rest of your life with. Someone who understands you. Someone who supports you, no matter what. Someone who helps you do your laundry.

Maybe you've already found the woman of your dreams. She's the type who isn't afraid to join your weekend football games (and can even throw a decent spiral). She thinks the tattered, paint-splattered sweatpants you wear to watch television are hot. And when it comes to sex, she understands that giving is just as important as receiving.

So how do you turn your best girl into your only girl? Before you strap on the knee pads and break out the Tiffany's box, you're going to need some pointers. After all, lucky guys do this only once. So make your own luck: Prepare. We'll show you how.

20 Things Every Man Must Do before Settling Down

Gonna take the next step? Make sure you haven't missed any. BY DANIEL LISTWA

1. Erase bad karma. Go back to your favorite bar—the place where you used to get so drunk that you'd throw chairs at closing time—and buy everyone a drink. Leave sober, all chairs in place.

2. Google your high school crush. Give her a call. After 15 minutes of bland banter, admit to yourself that you're not missing a thing.

3. Ask your parents for advice. And for once, take it.

4. Gather your three best friends and take a 2,000-mile road trip to Vegas. Or the Grand Canyon. Or any beach where exotic women wear clothes that could double as a chipmunk's eye patch.

5. Remember all that financial mumbo jumbo you never bothered to learn? It's time. Get someone to explain assets and liabilities, stocks and bonds, the W-2, the 1040, and APR. Open a money market account and start saving. It only gets more expensive from here.

6. Sneak backstage at a rock concert. Convince a groupie you're a lifelong friend of the lead singer. Use protection.

7. At the risk of going to jail, protest something you believe in. Causing a scene because Hooters abolishes 15-cent-wings night doesn't count.

8. Get a blood test. Just to be sure.

9. Quit a job.

10. Get fired from a job.

11. Sell peanuts in a ballpark. Or get hired as a golf caddy. In addition to living out a dream, you'll learn when to talk and when to keep quiet—the hallmarks of any good husband.

12. Find a job you love and want to do for the rest of your life. Take it, even if no one else understands. Eventually, they will.

13. Live with a female. Learn how to share the bathroom.

14. Read one issue of *Cosmopolitan*, *Self*, and *Glamour* magazines from cover to cover. That way, you'll at least know who's giving her those crazy ideas.

15. Baby-sit for 3 hours. Afterward, multiply the experience by 131,400. That's the number of hours the average man lives after having kids. Ask yourself, "Is it worth it?"

16. Test-drive a Volvo. You can't stop the future, but you can get ready.

17. Visit your doctor and have him perform a prostate examination. A responsible man is familiar with his prostate's health. This is how you get familiar.

18. If you have to cheat, cheat now. (P.S. You don't have to cheat.)

19. Get a gym membership and use it four times a week for a year. Then have someone take a picture of you. In a few years, you'll find a million reasons to avoid exercise. The photo will be a reminder why you should work out anyway.

20. Ask yourself, "Am I really the kind of guy who settles down?" Your answer might not be yes, but if you can't say maybe, then, brother, it's time for what she calls a big talk.

Is It Time to Say Goodbye?

Every relationship reaches the commit-or-quit moment.
Here's how to know if you should stay or she should go.

BY CHRIS CONNOLLY

THERE COMES A POINT, or many, in every relationship when a man thinks, "Should I stay or should I go? Commit to this something-or-other that's going pretty well, or search for another woman who might be better?"

I always chose go. Like most guys I know, I had a pattern: Date a woman for 6 months, maybe a year—then dump her. It wasn't that I didn't like the women I dated. I did. I just didn't want to commit to anyone. That's what I told the women as I cut them loose—and it's what I told myself. Until one day I decided to stay.

Once again, I'd been with a woman for a year. She's asked me not to use her name, so I'm going to call her, oh . . . Kirsten Dunst. Kirsten was perfect: blond, famous, signed to a six-picture contract. But something was about to come between us: specifically, two of my college buddies announcing their engagements on the same weekend. After receiving the happy news, I did what any single guy would do: I freaked out. "Where's my relationship going?" I asked. Lacking clear answers, I did what I'd always done—I went to Kirsten's house and told her it was over.

Fortunately, her experience dating arachnid-like superheroes had equipped Kirsten to deal with stressful situations. Instead of throwing things or kicking me out, she made a simple suggestion: "Why don't you try committing this time and see what happens?" That question, so clearheaded in the midst of emotional turmoil, triggered an immediate answer: "Yeah! Why don't I?" What if, this time, instead of leaving, I decided to commit? What would happen? I didn't know. I'd never done anything like that before. I promised to try, and, after I'd held Kirsten long enough to let her know I was serious, we did something suitably romantic: got burgers and rented *Happy Gilmore*. (Sigh.)

Unfortunately, Kirsten won't be there to stop you from going when you should be staying. The next time you reach a fight-or-flight moment in your relationship, consider these common triggers—they're not necessarily signs that you should bail.

NOT A REASON TO DUMP YOUR GIRLFRIEND, #1: OTHER WOMEN

STAY IF . . . the grass looks greener. Thinking about other women is to be expected. But if you think you're going to break up with your girlfriend and stumble into the arms of your soul mate, you're probably mistaken. "People are package deals," says Michele Weiner-Davis, author of *The Sex-Starved Marriage*. "If there are 10 things you love about them, there will be 10 things you hate about them." Sure, I'm not crazy about how Kirsten makes me do all the cooking and then never does the dishes, but I've learned to deal with it. And how do I know the hot ball girl at Putt-Putt Golf doesn't practice some weird religion and have six toes on each foot?

Other-woman thoughts may pop up more intensely when you're going through a rough patch in your relationship. "One easy mistake men make is comparing the middle of a relationship with the beginning," says Lee Baucom, Ph.D., a relationship coach and author of *Save the Marriage*. Before pulling the plug on a good thing, make sure

5 Times When She's Thinking "Stay Or Go?" by Nicole Beland

You're not the only one sizing up the relationship. She's most likely to ponder an escape from Coupletraz . . .

1. After so-so sex: The first time something goes awry in the sack (your stiffy goes soft, she can't orgasm, you fall out of her loft bed . . .) makes a woman wonder if the chemistry between you was fleeting. She'll ask herself how attracted she really is to you.

Make her stay: The more romantic and reassuring you are, the more likely she'll stick around after the sorry screw. To that end, put your arms around her and say something like, "I wish we weren't so off tonight, but I'm sure next time will be amazing."

2. During the big bash: It's the first time she's partied with your friends. This is an opportunity for her to see how you behave with your buds, how you deal with flirtatious women, and how you handle your liquor.

Make her stay: Introduce her as your girlfriend and give her lots of attention throughout the night, even though there are a million things distracting you.

3. When disaster strikes: Something horrible has happened to her, to someone she cares about, or to the world at large (think terrorist attack).

it hasn't just mellowed into something less electric but more enjoyable.

GO IF . . . you're standing on your neighbor's lawn. If you're cheating on your partner, there's a problem. Before you dismiss me as a master of the obvious, consider the many ways you can cheat. Clearly, there's the way that involves your secretary and a jar of marmalade. But there are more insidious types of adultery as well. Cheating is rooted in deception, not penetration. "Affairs aren't al-

Make her stay: Get to her side ASAP, or at the very least, call often to check on her. Leave her sad and solo during a rough time and she'll immediately be convinced that she can't count on you.

4. After her friend's engagement: As she eyeballs the new rock on her friend's finger, her mind will naturally wander to her own future wedding. Can she picture you at the altar, smiling lovingly as she promenades down the aisle? If she can't imagine being happy with you for a husband, she'll seriously doubt whether she should continue dating you. A talk about where your relationship is going is likely to follow.

Make her stay: Expressing a positive outlook—even if you're not making promises—is the best way to ward off her panic. Tell her you can imagine being happily married to her someday.

5. On her birthday: Turning a year older sends a girl into a stressful spiral of relationship reflection. Is she settling for you? Is your relationship as happy as it could be? Should she break up with you while she's still young and try to find Mr. Perfect?

Make her stay: She'll take the thoughtfulness of your gift as a sign of how well the relationship is going. Make sure it's personal—like a necklace with her favorite stone in the pendant, or a framed black-and-white photograph of her favorite city.

ways physical," says Baucom. "Sometimes emotional connections are even more damaging." Are you having this type of fling? Ask yourself these questions: Is there a person to whom I tell things I wouldn't tell my partner? Is there someone I'd feel guilty about having my partner meet? If you answer yes, you may be having an affair you didn't know about. And, my friend, if you're having an affair and not even getting any sex, you definitely have a problem.

NOT A REASON TO DUMP YOUR GIRLFRIEND, #2: FIGHTING

STAY IF . . . you fight right. I used to think that when I started fighting with a woman, the relationship was over. Not so. "Conflict is inevitable in a relationship," says Weiner-Davis. And it can be constructive. "It's how couples learn about each other and, if handled appropriately, tends to deepen and strengthen the bond," she says. If you're fighting with your partner, it means there's still passion, which is definitely a good sign. So how do you make sure you have the beneficial kind of fights and not the kind of shirtless brawls you see on *Cops*? "The best thing you can do is listen to your partner rather than plan what you're going to say next," says Weiner-Davis. "Simply saying, 'I understand,' and repeating back what you just heard can defuse a fight very quickly." Another reason not to break up just because there's fighting: It doesn't always end after the separation. My parents, for example, have been divorced for 20 years, and to this day, if they're in the same room together, all the plants die.

GO IF . . . You fight wrong. There's a limit to the amount of fighting a couple should endure. Sometimes you can simply do the math: Are there more bad days than good days? If so, then it may be time to go. Another way to have unconstructive fights is by not arguing at all. Holding everything in can actually be worse than having it out. "I'd rather work with an angry couple any day," says Baucom. "When both partners no longer care, there isn't much to go on."

NOT A REASON TO DUMP YOUR GIRLFRIEND, #3: UNHAPPINESS

STAY IF . . . your life sucks, temporarily. If your life's a seething ball of crap, congratulations! You may be lucky in love! Are you having a hard time dealing with work, your mother, that new pose in your yoga class? The difficulties you perceive in your relationship could derive from stressors that have nothing to do with your partner. A recent study of more than 100 people conducted by the State University of New York suggests that people with low self-esteem tend to question the strength of their partners' affections. If you're having personal problems, wait for them to cool before making a big relationship decision. Of course, you can also lean on your partner for support during times like these. "Once you recognize that you're letting personal problems affect your relationship, you can work with your partner to fix them," says Weiner-Davis. "Letting her know you're under stress will help her be more understanding, and often she can become a valuable ally."

GO IF . . . You're making your life suck. Are you trying to make partner at the firm, working out four times a week, taking a cooking class, volunteering at the shelter, and hosting a book club? Do you suppose this might be damaging your relationship? A study conducted at the University of Notre Dame, in Indiana, (so I read a lot of studies—so what?) showed that men who were extremely driven and fixated on success tended to have less-successful romantic relationships. If you're letting yourself fall into this trap, you may be purposely avoiding spending time with your partner.

NOT A REASON TO DUMP YOUR GIRLFRIEND, #4: COMMITMENT PHOBIA

STAY IF . . . you want to try. Just because you've thought about a breakup doesn't make it the right move. Do you want to try to work out the problems? If the thought of leaving causes you pain, there's a chance for reconciliation, says Baucom. When Kirsten made her proposal to me, I asked myself, "Will I change my life for this person? Will I give up highschoolgirldiscipline.com?" When I realized the answer

A MAN'S GOTTA DO

Percentage of all marriage proposals that are made by men:	Percentage of all divorces that are initiated by women:
82	44

was yes, I had to take the chance. Those poor high-school girls would just have to discipline themselves.

GO IF . . . you want to try a separation.

If you want to attempt a trial separation, you might as well just end the relationship now. It sounds harsh, but it's true. "Time apart is just a way to ease into a breakup," says Baucom. "You're trying to rebuild a relationship by minimizing the relating. That just doesn't make sense."

These signs aren't easy to read. But they may prevent you from getting stuck in a dead-end relationship, or pining over the one who got away. You might even find *Crazy/Beautiful* love. Just like Kirsten Dunst and me. By the way, we're now engaged. I asked her on the very same couch where I first decided to commit to her. After that, we did something suitably romantic: We got burgers and saw *Mr. Deeds*. (Sigh.) Go, Spidey!

A Prenup Pop Quiz

A diamond is forever. So before you propose, make sure you ask her these 10 questions.

BY TED SPIKER

MY BUDDY ED GOT DIVORCED because of golf, baked potatoes, and blackflies. See, Ed liked to play golf, which was no big deal—until he and his wife, Amy, started having money problems, and she'd remind him that he'd blown $500 a month "whacking a little ball around." Ed was also a slow eater, while Amy tended to gobble her dinner down rather quickly. By the time he'd buttered his baked potato, his wife had finished her meal and was up washing dishes, which was no big deal—except that it reminded them daily of how different they really were. Finally, Ed's job was transferred to Bangor, Maine, which was also no big deal—except that Amy was a Texan who, she said, "couldn't deal with blackflies," and, unlike Ed, came from a big, very close family whom she missed just a little too much.

These tiny hitches mutated into one festering, ugly, insurmountable problem, but that's not the really sad part about Ed's story. Instead it's what he asked me 10 minutes before he took his marriage vows: "Do you think I'm doing the right thing?"

He was asking me the most important question of his life, when all along, he should've been asking his future wife questions that would have given him the confidence to answer the important one himself.

Every marriage has difficulties. But there's something special about relationships that endure decade after decade—"the ones where people are celebrating their 50th wedding anniversaries," says

John K. Miller, Ph.D., a licensed marriage and family therapist at the University of Oregon. "They have the ability to communicate well enough to work out their differences."

The time to test your ability to do this as a couple is before you go diamond hunting. (Remember, 30 percent of marriages in the United States end in divorce.) To help you improve your odds, we asked scores of marriage therapists and both married and divorced men to suggest key questions you should ask her—and yourself—to gauge compatibility and to reveal potential hot spots in your relationship. Her responses to these topics don't necessarily guarantee bliss or blitzkrieg. (Though getting four or more answers that don't jibe with yours should give you pause.) It's how you resolve your differences that will guarantee a long and happy marriage.

MONEY

ASK THIS: What would you do if you won $100,000 in the lottery?

... TO FIND OUT THIS: Her financial priorities. "One of the biggest problems couples have is money and, specifically, differences in styles of spending and attitudes about their budget," says Karen Sherman, Ph.D., a couples' psychologist in New York City. You'll learn how she views money, saving, and long-term investing. Will all of it go toward cars and trips, or most toward retirement? It's not essential that you share the same investment strategies. What's important is using the conversation to prompt a discussion about financial behavior: how you pay bills, invest the year-end bonus, or decide on major purchases. If your attitudes don't mesh, now's the time to get the issues on the table and build a consensus.

DEGREE OF POTENTIAL DIFFICULTY: High

HER FAMILY

ASK THIS: What's your favorite holiday? How does your family spend it?

...TO FIND OUT THIS: Her family roots. Where you spend the holidays can be the biggest political issue since Trent Lott was interviewed on BET. "The underlying issue is whose family comes first, and that stands for who has the power in the relationship," says William Doherty, Ph.D., a professor of family and social science at the University of Minnesota and author of *Take Back Your Marriage.*

DEGREE OF POTENTIAL DIFFICULTY: Medium to high

RELIGION

ASK THIS: Do you believe in God?

...TO FIND OUT THIS: The compatibility of your faiths and religious rituals. In a Syracuse University study of 120 married couples, those who shared religious holiday rituals reported more marital satisfaction than the pairs who practiced holiday rituals separately. It's not necessarily the religion itself that's key—though the particular religion you practice can certainly be a huge issue with her family—it's all the things that go with it. "When you engage in celebrations and rituals, there's usually a lot of planning involved, something to look forward to that's meaningful to discuss," says Barbara Fiese, Ph.D., a professor of psychology and coauthor of the Syracuse study.

DEGREE OF POTENTIAL DIFFICULTY: Medium

HER WORK

ASK THIS: What's your dream job? And where would you most like to live?

...TO FIND OUT THIS: Her goals, and how far she's willing to go to reach them. Just asking shows support for her career, an important factor. A George Mason University study of 117 married couples found what the Wonderbra people have known for a long time: Those who felt they had more support had greater satisfaction than those who felt unsupported. It's also a good time to find out how far she's willing to move away from her family. "It's a very underappreciated area of stress—where are you going to live, whose family are you going to live near—yours or hers?" Miller says.

DEGREE OF POTENTIAL DIFFICULTY: Medium

YOUR WORK

ASK THIS: What was your dad's work schedule like?

...TO FIND OUT THIS: Whether she's already lived with a man who had the same work ethic and schedule as yours. Maybe her dad worked a 7-to-3 shift every day of his life, came home and played with the kids until they went to bed, and never worked weekends. Maybe he owned a business and set his own hours so he was always home for dinner. But your job—or your future job—may require late meetings, 60-hour workweeks, and business trips. And that can put stress on a relationship. "Working until 9, 10, sometimes later, night after night, is a constant source of stress with my wife," a friend of mine in publishing told me. "She still doesn't understand that this is the nature of the business at deadline time. It's not the life she was used to."

DEGREE OF POTENTIAL DIFFICULTY: High

INTERESTS AND DREAMS

ASK THIS: How do you envision your life in 5 years?

...TO FIND OUT THIS: Whether she wants to be a career girl, a stay-at-home mom, or a mom with a career. You'll also learn whether she expects to live in a big house in the 'burbs, an apartment in the city, or a farm in rural Kentucky. More and more research shows that the "opposites attract" notion is a myth. Successful couples usually have more similar priorities than not, says Leslie Parrott, Ed.D., author of *Saving Your Marriage before It Starts*. A couple has to have similar goals and a long-term plan, worked out together, to reach these goals. And even more important is a similar tolerance for risk and sacrifice. If you don't share the same values, they'll be a constant source of conflict in terms of how you spend your time and money.

DEGREE OF POTENTIAL DIFFICULTY: Medium

DISCIPLINE STYLE

ASK THIS: What do you think of spanking as punishment?

...TO FIND OUT THIS: Her thoughts on disciplining kids. We assume you've worked out whether you both want children, and maybe even how many. (You have done this, right?) But how you'll discipline them is a topic that's often overlooked. Bring it up the next time you see an unruly child at a restaurant shooting jelly packets across the booth. Ask her how she'd handle it and how she was disciplined as a child. "Either we tend to follow the way we were raised, or, if something was objectionable about the way we were raised, we do the opposite," Doherty says. Different parenting styles can cause the most strain on a marriage because they can be a daily, even hourly, source of conflict. "It's chronic acid on a relationship," says Scott Stanley, Ph.D., co-director of the Center for Marital and Family Studies at the University of Denver and coauthor of *Fighting for Your Marriage*.

DEGREE OF POTENTIAL DIFFICULTY: Medium to high

INSTANT SEXPERT

Single Minded

The National Marriage Project at Rutgers University interviewed 60 never-married men, ages 25 to 33. Their top 10 reasons for avoiding that walk down the aisle:

1. They can get sex without marriage more easily than in times past.

2. They can enjoy the benefits of having a wife by cohabiting rather than marrying.

3. They prefer to avoid divorce and its financial risks.

4. They want to wait to have children.

5. They resist change and compromise.

6. They're waiting for the perfect soul mate, and she hasn't yet appeared.

7. They face few social pressures to marry.

8. They're reluctant to marry a woman who already has children.

9. They want to own a house before they marry.

10. They want to enjoy single life as long as they can.

GENETICS

ASK THIS: What do your parents like to drink?

... TO FIND OUT THIS: Whether or not there's a history of alcoholism in her family. "Health problems like depression and alcoholism have a strong genetic component," Doherty says. "If her mother had depression or her father was a chronic alcoholic, there's a good chance it could creep up and become a problem." It's not a relationship killer (unless you use the terms "defective gene" or "your terminally plastered mother" when discussing it), but talking about hereditary health risks early will make it easier to discuss the same conflicts if they pop up in your relationship.

DEGREE OF POTENTIAL DIFFICULTY: Medium

IN-LAW APPROVAL

ASK THIS: How have your parents reacted to your previous boyfriends?

... TO FIND OUT THIS: If they'll think the current boyfriend is good enough for their little princess (and whether they'll pay big bucks for the wedding). "If her parents don't approve, there's a potential problem," says Sherman. Not that that's necessarily a deal breaker. Who are you marrying, her or them? What's more important is to learn something about your girlfriend by how she responds. Is she the kind of girl who only wants to please Mommy and Daddy? Or is she secure enough with herself to make her own life decisions? Here's a way to look for clues: Bradbury suggests asking how her parents have responded to her previous serious boyfriends, and then, if they disapproved, trying to elicit how she reacted to her parents' disapproval. Did they make a big deal over the last guy's prison record? Will they care about yours? If she supported her past boyfriends in exchanges with her folks, she's probably a keeper.

DEGREE OF POTENTIAL DIFFICULTY: Low to medium

FATHER FIGURE

ASK THIS: What is—or was—your relationship with your father like?

... TO FIND OUT THIS: Her attitude toward men. Especially toward the one who mattered most (before you). If her father was distant and cold, she may seek male approval. If her father was abusive or a cheat, she may have trouble trusting men. "If there's any unfinished business in her relationship with her father, it could manifest itself in your relationship," says Sherman. "When people get into serious relationships, they tend to look to their mate to give them everything they need. Couples get into trouble when they don't look closely at these tendencies early on." You also should consider her relationship with her mother, which could have the very same implications. If she can't pee without calling her mother to tell her all the details, that's not going to change after you walk down the aisle.

DEGREE OF POTENTIAL DIFFICULTY: Medium

AND THE MOST IMPORTANT QUESTION OF ALL. . . .

Finally, you need to ask yourself this: "Can I ask these questions and have an honest, intelligent conversation with this woman when we disagree?" Because if you can't, none of her answers really matter.

Confessions of a Perfect Mate

14 simple secrets to keeping her happy

BY HUGH O'NEILL

I AM THE BEST HUSBAND in the world.

If my wife were to read this, she'd fall to the floor, convulsed in laughter, and then gasp something about my "dazzling lack of self-knowledge." But no matter. I wear her ignorance of my excellence as a badge of honor. The best performers inhabit their roles; you never catch them acting.

I wasn't always a paragon. In my early years, I was a journeyman at best. In '88, I treated a precious marital secret as though it were the score of the Bulls game. And back in '96, there was a New Year's Eve kiss with our neighbor that probably should have been more perfunctory, less probing. But over the past decade, inch by inch, I've mastered the gig,

GOOD HUSBAND TALK

"I'm sorry. I'm an idiot sometimes."

and for the last few years, I've been locked in. I can see the seams on every chance to love, honor, and cherish. I'm in the husband zone.

According to my psychotherapist brother-in-law, the very ambition to be a perfect mate is destructive. "People aren't *perfect*, Hugh," is how he puts it, sounding amazed that a man can have reached my age and learned so little. Apparently, I have to outgrow my "habit of heroic thinking" and just aspire to be the best husband that I—

"flawed human that you are," is the way he put it—can be. I don't think he believes I'm the world's best husband.

I don't know how I got so good at this. As a kid, I had a front-row seat on my father's version of husband, which, at least according to my mother, was a star turn. And as a grown man, I've watched my father-in-law dazzle his sidekick of 53 years. But I have no formal credentials, and the only marriage counseling I ever got, from the rabbi the day before my wedding, amounted to "A Catholic and a Jew? Don't bother. Cancel the wedding and save on the divorce." My only qualification? I've been a husband for a long time—24 years according to the state of Pennsylvania, over 30 by common-law count—and, fortunately for you, I've made many, many mistakes from which you are about to learn. I've stumbled onto the secrets, and I'm willing to share.

BAD HUSBAND TALK

"I'm sorry if that made you feel bad."

I understand your skepticism. After all, what do I know about the unique and twisted deal you've made with your Mrs.? But I do know this: For all their variety, M-F relationships have lots of DNA in common, too. The challenge has little to do with the details of biography. Whether a man grows the wheat on the Great Plains or trades its futures on the Chicago Board of Trade, harvesting the riches of he and she is the same neat trick.

Will you ever be as great a husband as I am? Not likely. By now, I'm the gold standard. But you can do better, my brother. (And that's true for you unmarried guys, too: If you're with her, you can learn to be with her better.) I've condensed my wisdom into some guiding thoughts and tricks of the togetherness trade. Think of them as batting tips from Barry Bonds. Stash them in a part of your brain that guides your behavior, and two good things will happen: She'll get the partner she deserves, and you'll get the satisfaction and, oh yeah, the sex of which you dream.

THOUGHT #1: TAKE UP THE LANCE

The word "husband" doesn't generally conjure up heroic thoughts. Quite the opposite. It's freighted with connotations of little: the groom statuette on top of the wedding cake.

Purge all the mild-mannered associations with "husband" from your mind and put some swagger into the role. Imagine you're in one of those old castle movies. You're Sir Truth-and-Justice, bearing the colors of fair lady. Ignore the fact that you're actually drowsy and drooling on the 7:18 back to Philly; that's a fact, but not the truth. You're her champion, entering the lists on her behalf. Your quest? Oh, nothing big—just to enrich her experience of being alive. Don't worry. Yours gets juiced in the process. Pay no attention to small-minded men like my brother-in-law, Mr. Set-the-Bar-Low-and-Cut-Yourself-Some-Slack. Think big.

THOUGHT #2: WORK THE REUNIONS

You come though the door tired, maybe distracted about something at work. You riffle though the mail, ask her a routine how-was-your-day question, and give her a pro forma kiss. But let's face it, you don't really focus on her, do you? She gets only a small sliver of your attention. Not good enough.

Don't panic. I'm not about to suggest in-the-moment mindfulness. Men can't be "in" every moment. Besides, you can be a great mate without noticing every freakin' mote-filled shaft of sunlight dappling every damn dale. The secret is to "husband" your limited supply of attention, save it for deployment at pivotal times. Think like McEnroe, who would occasionally tank a forsaken fourth set, saving his strength for the fifth. Which are the key moments? The reunions. Each time you're about to be reunited

GOOD HUSBAND TALK

"I understand your feelings, sweetheart."

with the old ball and chain, take a few seconds and resolve to be fully tuned in during that *particular* come-together moment. You can do it. Trust me—if I can, you can. Here's the plain truth: For all the habituation of marriage, all the erosions that come with familiarity, a link between a man and a woman is also instantly renewable in a momentary locked-on gaze. For just a beat, maybe two, claim her with your eyeballs. Look at her in a way that says, "Okay, everything's fine now. I'm glad to be home, back in our powerful secret." This kind of subtle but daily maintenance keeps the engine thrumming.

> **BAD HUSBAND TALK**
> **"Yeah, well, my ex didn't think it was disgusting!"**

THOUGHT #3: KILL "NEVER" AND "ALWAYS"

When you and Lucy argue, don't use either of these two words. First of all, they're not technically accurate. It's not true that she *never* wears the cheerleader skirt; you got some boolah-boolah on your birthday. But, more important, they're gas-on-the-fire words. Instead of these indicting adverbs, use ameliorative words—like "sometimes" and "I feel" or "I wish." Darn right they're soft, but guess what? The best husbands actually are a skosh more sensitive to her feelings than your average brute of a mate. By the way, the words "always" and "never" are great when you're complimenting her, as in, "You *never* fail to amaze me," or, "I *always* enjoy reaching under the old pleated corduroy."

THOUGHT #4: LAUGH AT HER

Among the most affirming things one person can do for another is to laugh at the other's attempts at humor. Lots of husbands, over time, forget this salute. What's that you say? Your wife isn't funny? So what? Neither is your dolt of a boss, but you laugh at his lame attempts. Why? Because you're trying to prove you respect him. Bingo! One of the biggest dangers marriages face over time is that Marge and Homer stop trying to demonstrate their respect for each other. In fact, in some couples, even if her quips are funny, husbands don't laugh anymore. She craves that kind of easy endorsement—and deserves it much more than the slack-jawed con-

GOOD HUSBAND TALK

"If you died!? Jeez, I'd date Jack Daniels!"

niver who somehow managed to weasel a spot above you on the corporate flowchart.

Speaking of laughter: It stands for masculine exuberance that too often ebbs as a marriage, and a man, ages. The joyfulness of a man is one of the traits that womenfolk cherish in our kind. It's tonic for the woes that can worry a gal. Keep it on display.

THOUGHT #5: KEEP HUCK ALIVE

At the end of *Huckleberry Finn*, our hero vows to light out for the territory before the womenfolk can "sivilize" him. I'm not suggesting you flee; perfect husbands are always reachable. And when a man says, "I do," he implicitly agrees to tame some of his less polite urges in deference to womanworld. But beware of too complete a surrender. Huck's instinct to resist domestication is husband gold.

Too many husbands get feminized over the years. Often, because she's more organized than he is, lots of guys cede decision making to her and, bit by little bit, turn into their wives' assistants, guests in their own homes. You see this most often in older men who've been married 30-plus years, but it can happen in young husbands, too. Their slogan may as well be "Yes, dear." Here's a good indicator: Are there rules about where in the house you're allowed to eat? If so, you haven't tended the flame of Huck. Get feisty. Strain at the traces a bit.

It's vital that you stay male. Sure, gender roles are evolving. I understand—and with due

BAD HUSBAND TALK

"If you died? . . . Probably Julie. No, no . . . Wendy."

respect, yadda yadda yadda. This doesn't mean that you shouldn't cook, or that she shouldn't slap up paneling in the playroom; everyone should use all their skills. But you'll earn more respect for tending to *traditional* manly basement-and-garage stuff than you will for whipping up your zesty marinara sauce. Clean gutters get you husband points. Spotless dishes, not so much. Politically correct women will deny it, but you'll warm your wife's heart more by snaking out the drain in the kids' tub than you will by giving the kids a bath in same. Moreover, husbands don't care about thread counts or ottomans or the stuff hanging on the walls; if they do, they keep it to themselves. Don't get too "sivilised." Even a wife who conspires in the gelding of her guy often misses the stallion she diminished. She won't admire you for coming to heel; eventually she'll hold you in contempt.

THOUGHT #6: MAKE THE LION'S ROAR

Describing his important role during World War II, Winston Churchill once remarked that, though he was no lion, it had fallen to him to make the lion's roar. Every now and then, husbands have to get fierce, defiant on behalf of their team. It won't happen often, but when you're in a confrontational situation, where reason and soft words have failed—a dispute with a teacher, a vendor, a bill collector, your neighbor, your mother—be prepared to bark in unambiguous defense of your team, or fire off a "Don't mess with Texas." Don't shrink from this obligation. Her regard for you will shrink if you do.

THOUGHT #7: BE A LAMBYKINS

Yes, this contradicts the carnivorous idea above, but a husband is versatile; he can hammer the tee ball *and* feather the wedge. Softness and kindness and tenderness and all those traits that ain't much use in the marketplace are pure gold when it comes to being the man of the house. For lots of us, the hard part isn't being strong but being weak.

You know the slander about how we never ask for directions? Well, what our critics never mention is that we're not *allowed* to ask for directions. From the time we're boys, we're taught that real men know what they're doing.

> ## GOOD HUSBAND TALK
> **"Thanks, baby."**

The world and women don't admire guys who are uncertain. Which might explain why we're reluctant to admit anything's wrong, even when we're hemorrhaging—no, make that *especially* when we're hemorrhaging. We're fine. We're men. Why wouldn't we be fine? Whaddya think? I'm some kind of guy who's not fine?

The bulletproof charade doesn't make for good husbands. It's hard to love a guy who's always large and in charge, tough to hug a guy on a pedestal. Get weak, buddy. A good husband relies on his wife, values her counsel, trusts her to love him even though he's not in command. We're most human when we're wounded or lost. Mister Rogers once said that the best gift you can give somebody is to gracefully receive his help. That enriches everybody, giver and getter alike. Now and then, wrap your arms around your wife and whisper that you're a mite confused. Let her help you find your way.

THOUGHT #8: NOTICE HER NOOKS AND CRANNIES

When the Woody Allen heroine laments that our man is not as thoughtful and romantic as he used to be, he fires back that nobody can sustain the charm pace of courtship. "You could get a heart attack," he says. Funny, but not exactly true. One of the best things about women is that they don't demand much, at least not when it comes to the thoughtful husband gesture. Wives are suckers. It's heartbreaking so few husbands seize the chance to dazzle when so little attentiveness goes so far. You don't have to do something gracious every week; every 90 days or so will put you in the husband hall of fame.

Pay attention to the details of her. Now, I understand that attention and details are not our strong suits as a gender. But I believe you can do this, my brother. Try making a list of her enthusiasms, enumerating things she likes. Then, from time to time, demonstrate that you have a good working knowledge of her. Let's say she's an organization nut. If you see a set of nested plastic boxes at Target, score them for her. For only $6.99, you acknowledge, even endorse, her taste for stashing stuff. She a tennis player? A gardener? A collector of Mayan sexual devices? Whatever her particular pleasure, find a way to tip your hat to it every few months. Wives enjoy knowing that you see them specifically. Good husbands generally know all of the following: her favorite cookie, her favorite tea, and the color of her eyes.

THOUGHT #9: SHE NEEDS CLOSENESS TO FEEL SEXUAL; YOU NEED SEX TO FEEL CLOSE

This is the fundamental impenetrable puzzle of love. I have no idea what to do about this. But great husbands have it in mind at all times.

THOUGHT #10: BE TOUCHY

Apparently, we too rarely touch our wives—except, of course, when we're taxiing for takeoff. It pains me to cede any ground, but we're guilty as charged. I know one husband who, when he's feeling conjugal, actually touches his wife as though he

BAD HUSBAND TALK

"I said, 'I don't want to talk about it.'"

cherishes her character, when in fact he's hoping to cherish her caboose in a kitchen quickie. She sees through me every time. Did I say *me*? I meant *him*.

Nonsexual touch is a potent, underused endorsement of another soul. As you're heading out the door, giver her upper arm a quick, affectionate double squeeze. As she's walking by, try a playful pat on her moneymaker. Not a grab; the enthused, gentle swat of a teammate. As you're walking into a party or to your table, put a guiding hand, lightly but surely, on her lower back. If your pinkie ventures just far enough south to oh-so-barely tap the top of her bottom, it doesn't make you a pig but a protector.

Some nothing-special Tuesday night while she's standing at the sink doing the dishes, come up behind her and give her a kiss on the back of her head. It should be more than a peck—make it last 1.4 seconds. Throw in a little grunt of gratitude; its message is only this: "I'm a lucky man." Don't linger behind her. No arms. No hint of pelvic urge. She'll get cranky if she suspects you're cruising for dessert while she's scraping chicken gunk off a baking dish. Just drop the husband kiss on her noggin and get the hell out of there. She'll feel valued, which studies show is something people, especially female people, quite like.

THOUGHT #11: SEE THE TEACUP

The perfect husband understands that women often get confused by stuff that doesn't matter, as in the unwashed teacup that's been in the sink for 10 days. Few wives understand that it isn't that we *see* the teacup and *elect* not to rinse it, but rather that the neural link between our eyeballs and brains actually keeps us from *seeing* the cup. The gender biology of why we don't see the cup comes down to this: We have a lot of more important things on our minds. Would we have a shot with J.Lo? Will the Bills cover? Any chance of sex today? Is there a God? If so, why did he give J. Lo to that jerk Affleck? Our minds are cauldrons of profound thoughts. Any wonder we occasionally overlook some stray dishware?

GOOD HUSBAND TALK

"I was going to ask if you'd *lost* a little."

Charge: We don't help enough around the house. We're guilty. Even men who are domestic divas rarely do *half* of the housework. Thirty-six percent? Maybe. But 50 percent? Almost never. But here's the fix: Do more. Not a lot more—just a little more. One of the best things about women is that they really appreciate the smallest sign that you're trying. They're effort-oriented. Try walking into a room with a woman's mind. Imagine that your brain has space in it for trivialities like unwashed cups. Ask yourself: "If I were a psycho neat-freak, what would bother me in here?" The teacup—which sometimes takes the form of the kids' sneakers under the table or the metro section crumpled on the couch—will suddenly reveal itself to you.

BAD HUSBAND TALK

"I *like* you with a few extra pounds."

The hub who would be king occasionally does things not because they actually need doing *but because she wants them done*. Doing something for her makes you strong, not weak. It's counterintuitive, I know. But I swear, it's true.

THOUGHT #12: DON'T WITHHOLD YOURSELF

You've got a lot going on inside you—some of it quite scary. While I am not a proponent of telling her *everything* that's boiling around in there—enough with how eBay was your idea!—beware the husband tendency to get quiet over time, to assume that she either knows what you're thinking or is not interested. Remember, you're not as boring to her as you are to yourself, and marriages more often suffer from too little info transfer between him and her than they do from too much.

Sure, you have to do *some* editing, but air it out. Did you hear a song today that reminded you of the family trip that summer to Tricky Pond? Tell her. Not everything has to have some big meaning. The point is this: She's entitled to a reasonably authentic version of you, not some subdued version that makes you resemble every other Affleck drone out there. Be a particular, fully fledged person, not just some generic guy sharing space with her. The best husbands stay vivid.

THOUGHT #13: SHE AIN'T BROKE, SO DON'T FIX HER

People rarely change unless they feel accepted as they are. Once folks feel they're not *required* to change, growth happens.

THOUGHT #14: PLAY TO WIN

You know the athletic wisdom that warns against playing *not to lose,* that argues you have to be loose to let your skills flow and maximize your game? Same goes for marriage. Oh, sure, you can have a perfectly fine little partnership taking the cautious route. He & She Inc., may even hum along nicely if you companionably sidestep the brier patches. But that's no way to be a *great* husband. She's entitled to more, the full monty, the whole experience of being affiliated with—no, make that loved by—a man.

People often settle for accommodating coupledom because they're afraid some explosive issues will blow up the marriage. They fear ending their days alone, living under the bridge behind the high school. Set yourself free to play bravely by taking the big risk, divorce, off the table. Decide that you meant what you said at the wedding, that this woman, come what may, is your partner for life. Older couples often report that once they've gone past the point where they might leave each other, their partnership gets an invigorating second wind. No longer afraid of being alone, they talk things through. In pursuit of something richer than mere amity, they explore regrets, grievances. Sure, it can be difficult, but it's full and human and adrenal and, hallelujah, not dull. And it can lead to a more spacious marriage, a connection that is full-hearted, well-tempered instead of taped together.

QUICKIES

Dropping the L-Bomb:
Use It to Your Advantage

Saying "I love you" to a woman is a gamble—especially if you're dropping the L-bomb without a guidance system. We've done some reconnoitering, and nearly every woman told us she waits for the man to say it first. Here's how to make sure it doesn't blow up in your face.

Situation: Date 3

WIN, LOSE, OR DRAW: Lose

WHY: "An early I-love-you has more to do with fear than commitment," says Patricia Love, Ed.D., author of *The Truth about Love*.

WHAT WOMEN SAY: "My response: 'Psycho killer, qu'est-ce que c'est?' Run away," says Annie, 25, a social worker.

Situation: You're Exclusive

WIN, LOSE, OR DRAW: Win

WHY: By 6 months, "if you haven't said it yet, she's going to start wondering if the relationship is going anywhere," says Love.

WHAT WOMEN SAY: "Why hang around for one man to commit when there are a million more just like him I haven't seen naked yet?" says Amy, 24, a teacher.

Situation: You Wake Up Next to Her

WIN, LOSE, OR DRAW: Win

WHY: She's already gone to bed with you, so she won't think you have ulterior motives. She'll take it to heart.

WHAT WOMEN SAY: "First thing in the morning, when I look crappy and have dragon breath? Now, that's love," says Lynn, 24, an editor.

Situation: You're Fighting

WIN, LOSE, OR DRAW: Win

WHY: Context is crucial. "It's reassuring after a fight because it says, 'I am so sorry, because I do love you,'" says Love.

WHAT WOMEN SAY: "It's a major turn-on—the unconditional-love thing wrapped up with the whole high-intensity anger/heat/passion dynamic. Then we can screw like bunnies after making up," says Jennie, 31, a realtor.

Situation: During Sex

WIN, LOSE, OR DRAW: Draw

WHY: It doesn't necessarily mean anything. "If someone yelled out, 'Oh my God!' you wouldn't assume that person was a born-again Christian," says Love.

WHAT WOMEN SAY: "If a guy manages to pant out an I-love-you during sex, I dismiss it. For all I know, he's talking to himself," says Lynn.

Situation: You're Dumping Her

WIN, LOSE, OR DRAW: Lose

WHY: "It just gives her false hope," says Love.

WHAT WOMEN SAY: "For the next 6 months, I'll just ask myself why you're breaking up with me—or worse, stalk you with the question," says Chandra, 28, a bartender.

Situation: She's Dumping You

WIN, LOSE, OR DRAW: Draw

WHY: "If you do love her, it could work to your advantage. Maybe the reason she's breaking it off is because she doesn't think you really

---

SPLIT COMMITMENT

Percentage of single women who are looking for a long-term commitment or marriage online:	Percentage of single men who seek the same online:
48	39

care about her," says Felicia Rose Adler, author of *Master Dating: How to Meet and Attract Quality Men.*

WHAT WOMEN SAY: "I'd like to say that I wouldn't fall for this, but I'm sure I would," says Chandra

Situation: On the Phone or in Writing

WIN, LOSE, OR DRAW: Lose

WHY: It can work in a sincere love letter, but if it's casually tacked on to the end of a message, "It's going to make her wonder, 'Does he really mean that?'" Adler says.

WHAT WOMEN SAY: "The first time I actually heard that elusive phrase issue from my man's mouth, it was muttered at the tail end of a voice mail. Definitely not the most manly way to handle it. Yet, oddly enough, it still made my heart skip," says Deanne, 32, a publicist.

Situation: In Front of Other People

WIN, LOSE, OR DRAW: Win

WHY: You can't go wrong—even if she's embarrassed, she'll be impressed.

WHAT WOMEN SAY: "Sure, it's a true PDA. But it's not a bad thing. People who say 'I love you' only on their wedding day are missing out," Julia, 28, a journalist.

Situation: After You Cheated on Her

WIN, LOSE, OR DRAW: Lose

WHY: Don't feed her crap when you're up to your ears in it.

WHAT WOMEN SAY: "Don't feed me crap when you're up to your ears in it," says Lynn.

BEING TALL

A U.K. study of 10,000 people found that men who are over 5' 10" are not only more likely to find successful long-term relationships but are also likely to have more children during the course of their lives than shorter men.

ASK THE GIRL
NEXT DOOR The honest truth about women
from our lovely neighbor

The Wedding Zinger
**My girlfriend is always dragging me to weddings. How can I convince
her that she should go without me?** —M.M., BY E-MAIL

Get a horrible haircut, sprain an ankle, or come down with some nasty
stomach thing and lose your lunch on your only suit, because it's going to
take a hell of a good excuse to get you off the hook without a fight. No
matter how much you hate weddings, your girlfriend will hate you more
for making her sit alone at a table while all of her friends slow-dance with
their significant others under the twinkling lights of a chandelier. The
only thing worse than having to sit at the depressing singles table is
having to sit at the singles table when you're not really single.

Gimme a "P," Gimme an "I" . . .
**My girlfriend and I have been dating for more than a year, and I'd
really like it if she would go on the Pill so we can stop using condoms.
How do I talk to her about it?** —WILLIAM, HOUSTON, TEXAS

You've got to understand that going on the Pill is a big deal for a
woman. The Pill can make us fat; it can make us crazy. And unless a
woman trusts a man 100 percent, using non-barrier-based protection
can feel a little like playing Russian roulette with her health. So broach
the subject with sensitivity, and never after sex. She'll think you're
being critical of the sex. Just bring it up sometime when you're not in
bed. Ask what her opinions of the Pill are. Then, before she can answer,
quickly add that if she thinks it's too soon to talk about it, you'll understand. A complete lack of pressure on your part is key to hearing a positive response.

Crib Sheet

I cheated on my girlfriend. Should I tell her?   —SIMON, BY E-MAIL

Here's something I've learned about cheating: Every time I've gotten
some on the side, it was because the current relationship wasn't
honest or satisfying. Things ended pretty soon, whether I 'fessed up or
not. So take the fact that you cheated as a signal that something is
very wrong between you and your girl. If the relationship is worth
saving, figure out why you strayed and, yes, talk to her about it—even
though it's bound to get you kicked to the couch. Otherwise, do everybody a favor: Keep the bad news to yourself, break up with your girlfriend, and find someone you actually want to be committed to.

Any Given Sunday

**My girlfriend gets bent out of shape when I watch football on
Sunday. Why don't women understand that sports are really
important to guys?**   —F.C., KANSAS CITY, MISSOURI

I never used to understand what it was about certain sports that got
men into such a tizzy, but then I met a guy who took the time to go
over exactly what it was about the game (in his case, tennis) that was
so fascinating. He explained the scoring, the rules, the individual
players' backgrounds, and what made one shot more difficult to return
than another. By the end of his speech, I couldn't take my eyes off the
screen. It was probably similar to the way his dad or brothers got him
excited about watching sports when he was a kid. So the next time
your girlfriend is bitching about your Sunday obsession, why not per-
suade her to crash on the couch next to you for a quick lesson in the
glory of pigskin? It'll get her ready for some football.

For more honest answers about women, look for Ask the Men's Health Girl Next Door wherever books are sold.

HOT MONOGAMY

25 Ways to

To some guys we know, sex with the same person—night in, night out—sounds like a prison term. The fear of spending eternity in lockdown with one bunkmate is enough to make solitary confinement sound appealing. Monogamy doesn't have to be a Texas death sentence. Chances are, you are your own jailer, and all you need to escape are some lessons from the outside. To that end, we offer tales of some reformed no-good-nicks and a few more optimistic words on ditching the shackles without losing the girl.

Get ready; your life sentence is about to become a lust sentence.

23 Ways to Be Her Hero

Humble suggestions from a fair maiden

BY SARAH MILLER

1. You can put down the weights and the protein shakes. You might want us to be perfect looking; we simply want you not to be fat.

2. Replace all of those hideous size-extra-large T-shirts with something that actually sort of fits. We think you might be a medium.

3. Never allow anyone who listens to baseball on the radio to cut your hair.

4. Purchase white sheets that don't contain polyester.

5. Blue-book value isn't everything. Take the money you were going to spend putting the backseat DVD theater in your Honda and buy a nice pair of shoes instead.

6. We don't care what the plan is. Just have one.

7. Candles. They're so cheap and they're so effective.

8. When you give her a gift, include a card. You can spend less on the gift if you write something nice. Don't buy a card with a message in it, unless you're dating Danielle Steele.

9. She arrives home from work eager for attention. You arrive home from work eager for several beers and the *Simpsons–King of the Hill* hour. The moment you come home, hug her, look into her eyes, and say that you're happy to see her. This simple gesture, done with sincerity, will earn you lots of time on the couch.

10. Buy covered garbage cans for your kitchen and bathroom. They hide stuff we don't want to know about anyway.

11. Make a list entitled "Intolerable Behavior from Women," and when you see it happening, speak up. Let us know you won't be around no matter what, and we'll want to keep you.

12. Drive a stick shift. Men look ineffectual driving automatics.

13. Never utter the phrase, "I know I'm no Brad Pitt/Denzel Washington." You're a guy. Merely acting like you think you're hot makes you hot. Be grateful, because women actually have to be hot to be hot.

14. Short sleeves are for golf only; sandals are for Jesus only.

15. When a woman asks you to accompany her to a wedding or a family event, R.S.V.P. within 24 hours. If you find that you can't commit, do everyone a favor and break it off.

16. Stop operating on the in-trouble/not-in-trouble paradigm. Just because we're not yelling at you doesn't mean everything is okay.

17. If you're late, call.

18. Brush your teeth a lot.

19. Realize that if you "keep forgetting" to trim your nose hairs, we will "keep forgetting" to initiate sex.

20. If your television is of such a size that it's regularly commented on, hide it in a cabinet. You might have a penchant for (a) sloth, (b) passivity, or (c) tuning out the world, but she need not be reminded of this every time she walks into your living room.

21. You might not know what she wants you to get her for her birthday, but her friends do. Ask them.

22. When we're together, sometimes we're occupied with tasks— closing a window, putting on a new CD, petting the cat—that cause us to focus our gaze elsewhere. May we suggest these windows of time as the most favorable for scratching your balls.

23. Buy a Swiffer and use it. They come in dry (living room) and wet (kitchen and bathroom). Wash your dishes. Pick up your clothes. Swiff. She'll think you're a responsible adult.

Spite Club

How to fight with your wife and stay married

BY LAURENCE ROY STAINS

> "He who lives without quarreling
> is a bachelor." —SAINT JEROME

YOU SHOULD SEE A VIDEOTAPE of your last fight. No, not the one you had with that loudmouth at the Giants game. I'm talking about the argument with your wife.

Do you have any idea what you looked like? I do. I recently spent 3 days with some marriage experts watching couples fight. The arguments were all on tape, so I didn't have to duck any glassware being hurled across the kitchen, but the participants were real couples having real fights. And one thing became very clear: Fighting is a waste of time. Nobody wins. Everyone looks pathetic.

Every marriage has its disagreements, and we all argue about the same handful of issues (mostly money and kids, followed by housework, sex, in-laws, jobs, and time). That doesn't matter. What matters is how you argue. And if the pattern is destructive, it will surely kill a marriage. Bad feelings will crowd out good feelings until each partner feels like this: An opportunity to be with you is a chance to be hassled instead of loved and supported. That's the tipping point, when things turn sour.

And the Secret to a Happy Marriage Is . . .

Over the years, Markman and Stanley have found that the strongest couples have three traits in common.

1. They have the clearest sense of "us" as a team.

2. They're quick to fend off intrusions (such as family and outside demands on their time).

3. They talk more about the future. "They dream together. They take the long view," says Stanley.

Ninety-three percent of couples who fight dirty will be divorced in 10 years. This statistic comes from therapists who have investigated the causes of marital distress and failure. They videotape couples fighting; then they call these couples years later to see what happened. And what happened is shockingly predictable.

Two marital therapists who've conducted this sort of research at the University of Denver are Howard Markman and Scott Stanley. They now teach couples—both newlyweds and folks who've been married for years—how to fight better, how to clear the air without clearing the room. And they've been remarkably successful. Five years after participating in one of Markman and Stanley's courses, couples are twice as likely as couples who didn't take the course to still be together.

But you don't have to attend one of Markman and Stanley's workshops—or even read their book, *Fighting for Your Marriage*—to improve your relationship. Just start practicing these five strategies for keeping your arguments under control.

1. STAY OFF THE ESCALATOR

The first sign of destructive fighting is what Markman and Stanley call escalation. The idea is simple: Even though you and your wife may start out arguing about something small, inevitably your tempers flare, voices get louder, and that "little thing" disappears in an exchange of big threats.

To avoid such encounters, Markman and Stanley suggest a technique called "active listening," in which partners take turns talking and paraphrasing what the other is telling them ("What I hear you saying is . . ."). Yes, you'll feel dorky and self-conscious when you do this, but in a way, that's the point. Active listening slows you down, makes you listen to what the other person is really saying, and stops you from blasting away with both barrels.

Okay, so what if you're willing to stay on fighting's first floor, but your wife is the one constantly hopping on the escalator? Don't tell her to calm down. That just makes you come off as patronizing, which fuels her anger. Instead, you should make the effort to calm down. Keep your expression serious and say something like, "How about if I just listen to you for a few minutes, and you can tell me what you're thinking?"

2. BE HER MIRROR

Another sign that you're fighting ugly is invalidation. This occurs when you move beyond arguing about issues and start committing character assassination and name-calling. You know, the really fun stuff.

Lay off these tricks yourself. And if your wife slings one of those personal assaults your way, call her bluff. She's saying horrible things, but she doesn't really mean any of it. (If she did, she'd be gone by now.) Stanley suggests a very successful tactic that works in just about any contentious situation. "When someone's on the attack, paraphrase them. Gently reflect what she's saying so she can hear it." You could say, "Let me get this right. You think I've never really cared about you at all?"

Just be sure to sound sincere, not sarcastic. If you can do this, it's like holding up a mirror, which is gentler, and far more effective, than saying, "Look in the mirror, bitch."

3. DON'T DIS HER MEMORY

Often, in the heat of an argument, the first thing that each partner
will try to invalidate is the other's memory. If it turns into a who-re-
members-it-better shouting match and she says, "Oh, no, you said
blah-blah," don't respond in kind. You'll only imply that her memory
is more defective than yours (which it may be, but . . .). Instead, say
this: "I'm not sure what I said. What I meant was. . . . "

The point: It doesn't really matter who remembers it better.
"Bring it into the present," says Markman. "And stop arguing about
what was said or not said."

4. DON'T LET HER READ YOUR MIND

If she claims you were secretly hoping her mother wouldn't stay all
weekend, you could say, flat out, "Don't read my mind." But that's
risky. "You're labeling her behavior, and that could be dynamite," says
Stanley. Instead, try this: "That's not what I was thinking. Can I
please just tell you what I was thinking?"

You? Thinking? The shock might be so great that your wife will
drop her fighting gloves immediately.

5. DON'T PUT A SOCK IN IT

Withdrawal, which is Markman and Stanley's third fighting danger
sign, involves a clear and documented difference between the sexes.
Women value any interaction in a relationship, even if it's negative.
Men tend to value instrumental, problem-solving interactions, and we
shut down when the volume goes up. Our physical response to the
stress of yet another argument is the classic fight-or-flight reaction,
and most men take flight. Especially if she's the verbally skilled one
in the marriage—and most women have been a step ahead of us verbally since preschool.

All this leads to a lethal dynamic: She brings up a problem; you
don't want to talk about it. She gets angry; you fear more conflict and
close up tighter. She interprets that to mean you're detaching from

Rate Your Marriage

How perfect is your union? This eight-question quiz from *Fighting for Your Marriage* was devised by marital therapists Howard Markman and Scott Stanley as a quick checkup for marital health. Take this quiz by yourself and score each with a 1 (almost never), a 2 (once in a while), or a 3 (frequently). Then have your wife take the quiz. Compare total scores. Breathe deeply.

1. Little arguments escalate into ugly fights with accusations, criticisms, name-calling, or bringing up past hurts. Score: _____

2. My partner criticizes or belittles my opinions, feelings, or desires. Score: _____

3. My partner seems to view my words or actions as negative even though I didn't mean them that way. Score: _____

4. When we have a problem to solve, it is like we are on opposite teams. Score: _____

5. I hold back from telling my partner what I really think and feel. Score: _____

6. I think seriously about what it would be like to date or marry someone else. Score: _____

7. I feel lonely in this relationship. Score: _____

8. When we argue, one of us withdraws . . . that is, doesn't want to talk anymore or leaves the room. Score: _____

Total: _____

Total your scores individually. If both of you scored 12 or below, that's a marriage green light. You're in good shape. Scores from 13 to 17 are yellow-light scores—you need to be cautious about these warning signs. If your score is 18 to 24, that's a red light. You two had better stop and think about where your marriage is headed.

Were your scores very different? Women's scores are often a bit higher, says Stanley. "We always take the higher score as the one to be concerned about."

The average score on this quiz, by the way, is 11—on the verge of yellow. For more information, visit prepinc.com.

the marriage. For the past 25 years, this scenario has been noted by marriage experts for its reliability in predicting marital instability and divorce.

"The biggest mistake women make is getting angry at us," says Markman. It fails to solve the conflict and succeeds only in eroding the entire marriage. Here's what you can do about it. The next time you withdraw and she starts yelling about your pushing her away, say something like, "I don't want to shut you out. But I hate to fight with you." The exact words are unimportant. Just make her realize that you're not pulling away from her (the standard rap on men). You're just avoiding conflict. The first time you say this will be such a paradigm shift in your marriage, she'll be more affected by your change than the wording of it. In fact, your wife may be so stunned that the fight will stop right there. Makeup sex, anyone?

10 Women Who Hate Me

He loved, he lost, he learned. So now you can skip
steps two and three and proceed directly, happily ever after,
to number one.

BY MICHAEL LEWITTES

THERE'S A FELLOW IN MY TOWN who enjoys a vigorous, care-free love life with a plenitude of available women. Many of these women, in fact, are ex-girlfriends, but they happily welcome him into their beds whenever he wanders into their part of town. This fellow's ability to charm a woman and then break free of her spell makes him a happy man.

I am not a happy man. My ex-girlfriends do not welcome me back into their arms whenever I arrive in town. Taking up arms would be more like it. If I had a dollar for every time a woman slammed down the phone on me, I'd have . . . well, I'd have a pretty solid stake in the telecom industry. Indeed, the hardest part of writing an article called "10 Women Who Hate Me" has been narrowing it down to just 10. And just as each and every woman is unique and special in her own right, so too are the ways in which I've managed to piss them off.

So consider this a dig into the archaeology of attraction, and let's hope one of us starts to learn from my mistakes. (Names have been changed to protect the guilty. That would be me.)

1. ALEXA

About 10 years ago I had my own column at a large daily newspaper. It was exciting, but it was a lot of work. Unfortunately, the same could be

Exit, Loving

Just because there's no more "us" doesn't mean you can't get together for a little "he and she." Here's how to leave and still be loved, not loathed.

Let her see the breakup coming. A sudden breakup will leave her feeling abandoned and scarred. Preface your impending unpairing with light comments about how you're "no good at relationships" and how she'd be "better off with someone else."

Afterward, stay in touch. A friendly e-mail every week or so is more effective than swinging into town and trying to hook up.

Act like you don't care about the sex. If anything, joke that it had better not be on her mind, because you're not that kind of guy. Explain that you've decided to swear off physical intimacy for a while. She'll take it as a challenge.

Provide counsel. She needs advice on dealing with the landlord, the family, the new boyfriend? You're there to listen. "Just friends" is the vibe you want to give off.

Be discreet. If she's willing to be in touch with you after the breakup, she's really putting herself out on a limb, emotionally. Don't let it get back to her inner circle that you two are occasionally banging boots.

Keep it light. Sure, the possibility of reuniting is always in the air, but don't hint at getting back together for real. She'll hate you for it.

said about Alexa. I was young then, and like a lot of young guys, I was obsessed with proving that I was going to be somebody. To me, it didn't feel as though I was worthy of a woman's love unless I "made it." Indeed, I was so busy making it that Alexa ran off and made it with some other guy just for the company. Sure, I had chosen spending time at work over spending time with Alexa, but what choice did I have?

LESSON: It's not really a question of choosing between a woman and work. It's a question of choosing between a woman and yourself.

Like booze, gambling, or the tube, work is what you throw yourself into when, deep inside, you're more important to yourself than she is.

2. SHARON

Then there was Sharon, a lawyer I briefly courted. This one I was nuts about, so I made sure I was there when she needed me. To move furniture, for example. Or help with the laundry. Or feed her cat. I thought she'd see that I was the best boyfriend a woman could want. Actually, I turned out to be the best boy *friend* a woman could want. One day I just told her I felt like I should change my name to Matt and spend my days lying in front of her door.

LESSON: In love, never forget the rule of supply and demand: The more available a commodity is, the less people want it. Or, as my friend Eric says, "If you want a woman to come to you, back up."

3. CINDY

Cindy was a deeply religious woman who was saving herself. Let's just say we had drinks together at some point, and one thing begat another. The next day, when I confessed I wasn't really interested in a relationship, there was hell to pay. (She seriously hates me.)

LESSON: In the course of your dating life, there will be women who'll accuse you of being a jerk. Some of them will be right.

4. LISA

Lisa was smart and supportive and sensual, and we dated for nearly 2 years in college. Yet as terrific as Lisa was, I always thought there was a chance I could do better. So I broke up with her. Within 2 weeks I was out of my mind missing her. She was creative, she was compassionate, she had a different-colored thong for every day of the week. I must've been insane! I begged Lisa to take me back, which she did after a month of solid coaxing on my part.

About 2 weeks after that, I realized I'd made a horrible mistake and promptly broke up with her again.

LESSON: On a certain level, you always value what you've lost over what you have. So if you're going to end it, imagine first what you'll feel like knowing you no longer have that person's love, or support, or thong panties lying on the floor. Don't make any decisions in a relationship unless you're 100 percent sure and are ready to deal with the consequences, such as having that person never speak to you again or take a banner that says "I hate Michael Lewittes" to every college football game.

5. NATASHA

Natasha was a photographer. In a dark room, things between us developed quickly. In the light of day, however, I instinctively knew that we were too different. She was a militant vegetarian who loved animals more than people.

I love animals too, mostly broiled, but fried sometimes, with a little tartar sauce. I knew there weren't any long-term possibilities, so I surreptitiously played the field. One night when Natasha was out with her parents, I met up with another woman. At a steak house in New York, I shared wine and kisses with sexy Suzy until I heard, "Mom and Dad, this is Michael, my ex-boyfriend."

LESSON: Find out first if your girlfriend's parents are also militant vegetarians. And, oh yeah—don't cheat. If you really don't see a future, try playing the "Let's see other people" card; she may end it, but at least she won't hate you. Get caught cheating and not only will she despise you, but the other girl will, too.

6. SUZY

See above.

BAD MOVES MADE WORSE

Percentage of women who don't use a condom when they cheat:

37

7. ALLY

Once I was on the receiving end of the "Should we see other people?" ploy. Her name was Ally, a beautiful schoolteacher who was 6 years my senior. After a few months, Ally asked, "Do you think maybe we should keep this relationship open?" Even though I didn't think we should, I figured that's what she wanted, so I naively said yes. Uh-oh, test question, wrong answer. No matter how hard I backpedaled for the next few weeks, she had become convinced that I was a player, too much of an immature jerk to really know how to be serious about a woman. Which I wasn't. At least, not back then.

LESSON: "Open" and "relationship" don't go together in the female lexicon, and if a woman brings up the two words at the same time, it means she wants to either (a) make the relationship exclusive, or (b) end it. In a sense, the courtship and relationship phases are entirely different; once the two of you are together, she'll be looking for you to move the ball forward. So if you really want it, run with it, boy.

8. NATASHA'S ASSISTANT

Fortunately, Natasha the photographer didn't see everything in black and white, and she gave me another shot when I showed her my negatives—literally. Outside her apartment after the infamous "steakhouse affair," I arranged several feet of film to spell out "I'm sorry." She accepted my apology, and for 2 months I was happy. By month 3, I was feeling a very familiar itch, however, and by month 5, I was vigorously scratching it . . . with Natasha's photo assistant.

LESSON: I've strayed, and I've also been faithful, and I think I've figured something out: If you're (a) enthusiastic about the future, (b) able to give as well as receive, emotionally, and (c) confident in her fidelity, then you're likely to feel confident in your own fidelity. If you waver on any of those three, either fix it or get out; otherwise, you might as well make the motel reservations now.

9. JANET

Janet and I dated for a few months before we both realized that life together was nice, but nobody was going to confuse it with an epic love story. Still, even when the breakup is mutual, it takes a while to get over a woman. A few weeks later, I found myself at a big dinner party where a legendary Hollywood lothario was one of the guests. "The best way to get over a woman," he told a bunch of us, "is to get under another one." The next night I called up a woman who in many ways reminded me of Janet—because she was her best friend, Missy.

LESSON: A gentleman protects his ex's ego. Janet assumed that I had been more interested in Missy all along, and that I'd used her to get to her friend. Even after a cordial breakup, Janet is still so angry she makes my throat clench whenever I see her. Missy, she forgave. No surprise.

10. WENDY

The girl was beautiful, an Ivy League grad whose eyes sparkled with benign intellect and whose body seemed sculpted by the very hands of Mother Nature herself, and the moment we met, I knew she was a woman I could not resist. And I didn't.

Unfortunately, she wasn't Wendy. Wendy's the one I was dating and two-timing at the time.

So I did what guys do when they want to get out of a bad situation: They ignore it and hope it goes away. After about 3 weeks of broken dates and unreturned phone calls, Wendy finally got the hint. What I got was a big MasterCard bill, as Wendy had found one of my receipts in her dresser drawer and managed to order half of Amazon's inventory on my tab. (I think she saved the company.)

LESSON: If you're dating someone, even if it's only been a short while, you owe her the courtesy of a delicately worded, face-to-face breakup. Not "Sorry, Wendy, but I got a better offer."

A Night to Remember

There are moments in a man's life when good, wholesome sex becomes something more. When the bed rocks, the walls shake, and the wildlife starts howling at the moon. Rest up, 'cuz tonight's going to be one of those nights.

BY TED SPIKER

I **LIKE TO THINK OF A MAN'S SEX LIFE** as the 11:00 P.M. *Sports-Center*. Besides a few bloopers and vital stats (97 seconds—a career high!), we keep a reel of sexual highlights—maybe it's our first home run, or an incomparable breast stroke, or that dramatic come-from-behind victory.

But what exactly makes the difference between a decent sex highlight and one you'll replay your whole life? Depending on your preferences, it can be anything: urgent, sweaty, passionate, anonymous, long, short, in a cab, under a palm tree, with a palm tree, whatever. The defining characteristic is that it's just a heck of a lot better than the other 147 times you had sex this year.

Inspired to make more highlights, we pulled together a list of the eight most monumental sexual experiences in most men's lives and figured out why they're such milestones. The key in almost all of these instances is this: The hotter you make her, the hotter the sex will be. "A bonfire doesn't start instantly," says Lou Paget, author of *The Big O*. "You have to fuel it; you've got to light it." So here—in an effort to make once-in-a-lifetime experiences come more often—we provide the firewood and the gas. Your job: Light the match.

WEDDING-NIGHT SEX

WHY IT'S MONUMENTAL: It's her perfect day. She looks gorgeous (and she's been told that 493 times an hour). Her whole family is around her. And now she truly feels the comfort and security of having a husband. Translation: "The reward system in her brain is going bonkers," says Helen Fisher, Ph.D., an anthropologist at Rutgers University and author of *The First Sex*. Physiologically, her feel-good chemicals—dopamine and epinephrine—are firing fast, meaning she's wired to feel euphoric and to give as much pleasure as she's receiving.

HAVE IT TONIGHT: Even if you went on your honeymoon 12 years ago or don't plan on going on one for another 12 years, you can create the spark by triggering her reward system. Try these tricks:

- In the morning, use a ballpoint pen to write a sexy note somewhere on her body. Try the top of her thigh (prime real estate, with minimum exposure to coworkers). "Women are turned on by words," Fisher says. Start with "I," end with "you," and use the verb of your choice in between. Giving her 9 or 10 hours to see, think about, and fantasize about your note starts the percolation process.
- When she comes home, try this move. While facing her, hold her head with both of your hands, tilt her head back, and gently kiss the side of her neck. "If you touch a woman the way she wants to be touched, she'll be all over you," says Paget. That means staying away from your traditional "go to" spots and kissing the parts of her body you usually ignore, like the back of her hand, the inside of her elbow, or her hipbone.
- Now that you're under the covers, expand your repertoire of oral sex—a nice reward in itself. Paget suggests the Kivin method: You lie perpendicular to her body, which allows you to stroke her clitoris with your tongue in a crosswise motion,

rather than up and down. She'll appreciate the change in stimulation—hopefully, enough to return the reward.

HONEY-I'M-HOME SEX

WHY IT'S MONUMENTAL: If you haven't eaten all day, you pig out at dinner. Same with sex.

If you're attached, a business trip equals massive sexual deprivation. It means the closest thing you're getting to regular sex is the midnight showing of the hotel's $14.99 adult movie. (Note: Titles do not appear on your bill.) So when you reach home, the deprivation turns into sexual gorging. "You usually find that this is the most romantic sex, because it starts out with long, luscious kisses that really get the juices flowing," says Ava Cadell, Ph.D., a California sexologist and author of *Stock Market Orgasm*.

HAVE IT TONIGHT: You can simulate this kind of passion—whether you've been away for 8 days or 8 minutes—by giving her this kind of kiss, and in this order.

- Kiss her face all over—lightly.
- Lick the outside of her lips.
- Kiss her bottom lip. "There's a correlation between a woman's bottom lip and her vagina. Sucking gently on her lip will make her vagina swell," Cadell says.
- Gently suck her tongue. Cadell says, "I call kissing facial intercourse—it's really erotic."

A CANON IS FOREVER

Percentage of women who would rather receive a digital camera than diamond earrings:

SOURCE: Consumer Electronics Association Research Alert, 11/15/2002

MAKE-UP SEX

WHY IT'S MONUMENTAL: You yell, you scream, you break some dishes. Then you make up and head right to the bedroom, where there's more screaming. But this time, the only thing you're both breaking is the sound barrier (and maybe the headboard). "When you fight, anger drives up testosterone in both men and women. If you go to bed with increased testosterone and agitation, the sex drive is going to be stronger," Fisher says. "And more fantasies may flood your mind, which increases stimulation."

HAVE IT TONIGHT: You can reenact fighting—and the emotions that go along with it—without hurting each other, Cadell says. She suggests trying anything that will create a little physical tension between the two of you. Like . . .

- Miniature golf. "You can do anything that's just a little competitive," says Gloria Brame, Ph.D., a clinical sexologist and author in Atlanta. "Once you start competing, you can get physical and really work each other up."
- Pillow fights. "It starts her hair flying and her breasts moving, and even gets her gasping a little for breath," Brame says. "There's something very sexual about that."
- Naked wrestling. Hint: Let her win.

BREAKUP SEX

WHY IT'S MONUMENTAL: It's like the day before a diet. Tomorrow I'll start, but today I'm going to enjoy one last order of chicken wings. You've decided together that the relationship isn't working, but what the hey, one last tryst won't hurt anyone.

And it winds up being better than any you've had in the past 6 months for two reasons. One's physical: Fisher says that there's some speculation among researchers that in so-called last-chance copulation, a man may unknowingly alter the levels of certain hormones in his semen, and that may trigger his partner to ovulate spontaneously. In other words, your subconscious may try to hold on to the commitment by potentially impregnating her, even though you don't want to. The other reason is psychological: "When you know you're never going to see someone again, you want to leave her wanting you—and you'll do anything to drive her out of her mind," says Cadell. "So you both end up concentrating on being uninhibited."

HAVE IT TONIGHT: To make a woman less inhibited, try to reduce her tension, says Brame. Try releasing it in her body—and in her brain.

> • Clean out the refrigerator (or anything that shortens her to-do list). Showing thoughtfulness and initiative will make her a more willing sex partner, says Paul Joannides, author of *Guide to Getting It On*. While researching his book, Joannides talked to a female "escort" who had a valuable insight about her customers: "She said, 'I don't get it. These guys would get a lot more sex at home if they'd spend their money on a maid or cleaning service rather than spending it on me.'"
> • When massaging her, focus only on her earlobes, hands, and lower back—the unsung erotic spots. Hit the lower spine not only because that's where she stores a lot of tension, but also because you'll reach her pleasure zones in a more indirect path. Brame says, "This area is a nerve center with connections all over, so rubbing her lower spine could make her feel tingly in front."

BIRTHDAY SEX

WHY IT'S MONUMENTAL: It's clear who's doing the giving and who's doing the receiving—which means there's no pressure for the receiver to reciprocate, says Cadell. Because of that, there's a huge buildup of anticipation for the birthday boy. I wonder what she's going to give me this year!

INSTANT SEXPERT

Gild the Lily

This may be overkill, but sometimes that extra something is necessary. The site Speakingroses.com will deliver flowers embossed with your message in gold lettering on every bloom. Make sure you spell her name right. $70 a dozen

HAVE IT TONIGHT: For the 363 days of nonbirthday sex, you need to build that same anticipation between the two of you. You do it for her = she'll do it for you next time. Try this:

• Tell her you want to take her somewhere special tonight. Then ask if she'll leave her underwear at home.

• Take her to a place that plays Latin music. "Latin dancing is very sexual, especially the movement of the pelvis," Cadell says.

• When you're back home, you can give her your present: the ultimate mind-blowing orgasm. Have her get on top of you and tilt her hips forward a little so that her clitoris hits your pelvis. The tilting also means your penis will hit her G-spot. Those two spots will be plenty, but for extra pleasure, seek out and caress or lightly stimulate other sensitive areas—her lips, her nipples, her bottom—with your hands or fingers. The goal: sensory pleasure. Work as many angles as you can dream up; she'll let you know what's working.

FIRST-TIME-WITH-HER SEX

WHY IT'S MONUMENTAL: "It's exciting because of the discovery quotient," says Louanne Cole Weston, Ph.D., a licensed marriage and family therapist in California. "You're really tuned in to every sense, and you're feeling things for the first time." Another factor: Many men, especially those in long-term relationships, create a formula for what sex should be like. When that formula changes—as it often does with a new woman—it heightens excitement.

HAVE IT TONIGHT: Maybe it's not your first time with her, but your 501st. The key is playing with your senses—or at least stimulating them in a new way. "When you take away one of the senses, the others work overtime," says Cadell. Here are a few ways to change the sensory experience.

- Try Cadell's honey game: You're blindfolded; she hides a dab of honey somewhere on her body. You try to find it—using only your tongue.
- Take a swig of champagne, then kiss her body while it's still in your mouth. The fizz will tingle.
- Tie each other's feet together with her pantyhose. Mild bondage heightens sexual urgency, Paget says.

VACATION SEX

WHY IT'S MONUMENTAL: First, you're free from all the things that stress you out—the job, the bills, another late-season Red Sox fold. But the second reason Aruba sex is hotter than subdivision sex is the change in scenery. "There's a marking-the-territory factor for most men and women," Weston says. "Sex on vacation is a virginal experience in a way."

HAVE IT TONIGHT: From the simple to the extravagant, you can take a vacation day any day (boss be damned!):

- Turn upside-down on the bed—feet at the pillow end. "Even doing something simple like hitting the bed at a different angle or sitting or standing up on the bed will add extra stimulation," Weston says.
- Change the order of foreplay. "Remove the dip test from your repertoire," Paget says. "Any woman hates the kiss, kiss, kiss, tweak, tweak, tweak the nipple, dip, dip, dip to see if she's lubricated. That's a major turnoff." Instead, try kissing her neck, her inner thigh, then her pinkie finger or wherever else.

Move up and down her body like Ray Charles on ivory so she doesn't know where you're going next.

• Check into an adult motel on your lunch hour. "That's a pretty short vacation," Cadell says. In Los Angeles, a hotel called Splash features Jacuzzis in themed rooms that you can rent by the hour. But you can go to any hotel, then serve her lunch. "One study showed that black licorice increases blood-flow to her genital area by 40 percent, but any food that's phallic can be an aphrodisiac for her," Cadell says. Save room for dessert.

LET'S-HAVE-A-BABY SEX

WHY IT'S MONUMENTAL: Many couples feel an intense emotional connection the first time they start trying to have a baby. "For some, it's a very primal experience," Weston says. "For so long you've avoided pregnancy, but now you're ready to be a dad. Saying you want to have a baby with someone is very romantic."

HAVE IT TONIGHT: Start this way.

• Put flower petals on the top of a ceiling fan. Turn it on when she lies down.
• Have sex side by side. It's the most equal of the sexual positions. If you're facing each other, there's more of an emotional bond than when one is on top of the other, Weston says.
• Play your wedding song in the background. "If something has special meaning to you both, bring it to the bedroom because it creates a special connection between the two of you," Brame says. "Hopefully that special connection isn't a bottle of Jack."

Getting None

Sex is an American obsession. Yet an estimated 20 million men
are stuck in no-sex or low-sex marriages. If you're one of them,
here's how to revitalize your relationship.

BY JOE KITA

TOM IS A HEALTHY, HANDSOME, 40-year-old engineer. He's
been married for 12 years and has three sweet kids, plus a sprawling
house in the Atlanta suburbs. He seems the quintessential man-in-
full, except that Tom hasn't been laid in . . . "well, let me see if I can
remember," he says. "Oh, yeah, February 14, 1992. That's the last
time my wife and I made love. Before we were married, sex was pretty
frequent. Afterward, it became once a week, then once a month, and
eventually it just stopped. I've attempted to initiate romance and
been turned down so often I've quit trying. Don't get me wrong: I
love my wife. I wouldn't have stuck it out this long if I didn't. Have I
ever thought of having an affair? Sure, but I wasn't brought up that
way. The vows I made on my wedding day are sacred."

Tom is just one of hundreds of guys we heard from after posting
a note on the *Men's Health* Web site about no-sex or low-sex marriages. Some replies were of the grin-and-bear-it variety. Matt, for in-
stance, a 32-year-old plant manager in Milwaukee, wanted to know if
once every 2 weeks was little enough to qualify. "My wife and I had a
great night of passion last Saturday," he says, "but I'd just installed a
dishwasher earlier in the day. I feel like our sexual relationship has the
puppy syndrome: I poop outside, I get rewarded."

Other replies, however, were heart-wrenching. "My wife and I rarely have sex," says Nathan, a 38-year-old history teacher in Toronto. "She's committed to me and the kids, but she has no time for romance and little interest in sex. I've asked her why, but she's uneasy talking about it. So imagine my surprise when I came home from work on my birthday and she told me the children were spending the night with relatives. After a romantic dinner, she suggested we go to bed early. I felt like a kid about to get his first kiss. As I slipped beneath the sheets, she handed me a card that read: 'Your birthday gift is Channel 454, the Playboy Channel.' With that she rolled over and said, 'I'm tired. You can do whatever.'"

Not every married guy wants more sex. "The problem isn't my wife; it's me," says Gregg, a 35-year-old attorney in San Antonio. "I wake up every morning at 4:30, exercise, go to work for 10 hours, get home, play with the kids, then collapse into bed by 9:30. Frankly, at this point in my life, I value rest more than sex."

"I lost my desire to have sex about a year and a half ago," admits Eric, a 40-year-old assembly-line worker in Detroit. "At first I chalked it up to working the swing shift and being tired. But eventually I realized that even though I'd wake up with an erection, very little ever woke up my penis during the day. My wife has been supportive, but how do you tell someone you love and find attractive that you just aren't into sex anymore? I'm still physically capable, but I don't have the desire. Come July, it'll be 2 years since we made love."

What's going on here? America is supposed to be the most oversexed country on Earth. There's more sex in the media than ever. Any fetish you can imagine is a key-tap away on the Internet. Belly shirts are in. Boobs are out. If the United States had a sex gauge, it would certainly be needling past full. Wouldn't it?

"Despite all the allusions to sex that surround us every day, there just isn't as much sex going on as people think," says Daniel Stein, M.D., medical director of the Foundation for Intimacy, in Tampa, Florida. "Studies show that 45 percent of married couples have sex

Test Your Marriage

Find out if you're in a sex-starved relationship by taking this true-or-false quiz.

___ **1.** Sex is more work than it is play.

___ **2.** Touching always leads to intercourse.

___ **3.** Touching takes place only in the bedroom.

___ **4.** I no longer look forward to making love.

___ **5.** Sex does not give me feelings of connection and sharing.

___ **6.** I never have sexual thoughts or fantasies about my partner.

___ **7.** Sex is limited to a fixed time, such as Saturday night or Sunday morning.

___ **8.** One of us is always the initiator, and the other feels pressure.

___ **9.** I look back on premarital sex as the best time.

___ **10.** Sex has become mechanical and routine.

___ **11.** My partner and I have sex once or twice a month at most.

If you answered "true" to five or more statements or to number 11, or both, you're in a low-sex or no-sex relationship. If you've been married for 3 years or less, divorce is likely because you don't have much of a history of shared pleasure to help you pull through the low spots.

Reprinted with permission from *Rekindling Desire: A Step-by-Step Program to Help Low-Sex and No-Sex Marriages*, by Barry and Emily McCarthy.

one to three times per month. Thirty-three percent have sex zero to three times per year. And only 8 percent have sex four or more times per week."

"In my practice, I'm seeing more and more of what I call celibate relationships," says Lana Holstein, M.D., author of *How to Have Magnificent Sex*. "Typically, these are couples who have lost the magic, the urge to merge. Their pace of life has increased so much that they're living on the edge of exhaustion. That leaves very little time for true loving."

Determining whether or not you're in a sex-starved relationship isn't as simple as tallying the number of times you do it. Sexual satisfaction involves much more than frequency. That's why twice a month is plenty for some couples, while twice a day is barely enough for others. To put your marriage to the test, take the quiz on page 185. But keep in mind that there's a natural ebb and flow to sexual relationships as a result of pregnancy, illness, raising children, and stress. For a situation to be chronic, it must persist for at least 6 months. If your test score proves you're not scoring enough, don't panic. Experts say the first step to correcting the problem is realizing you're not alone.

"I've been a marriage therapist for 20 years, and I'd estimate that one in three couples struggles with this issue," says Michele Weiner Davis, author of *The Sex-Starved Marriage*. "It affects all types of people, regardless of age or years spent together. It's America's best-kept secret."

This last statement is especially true for men. While it's become cliché for women to complain to their girlfriends about oversexed husbands, for a married guy to admit to his buds that either he's not getting any or he no longer desires it is still too painful. It's almost easier to admit to a sexual dysfunction. Indeed, that's why we had to disguise the identities of the men we quoted. No one would speak to us on the record.

Holding this kind of shame and resentment inside eventually results in a "gridlocked relationship," says Dr. Stein. "The partners function as parents, as breadwinners, as housekeepers, but they're more like brother and sister. Not only does the frequency of intercourse decline, but so does the kissing, hugging, and touching. Love wanes under these circumstances. A relationship is a living thing that requires nourishment to grow. And that nourishment is sex."

Aaron, a 32-year-old architect in Santa Fe, describes it this way: "My wife's lack of desire has created tension between us. If I press the issue and she still doesn't want to have sex, then she feels bad for saying no, and I feel bad for forcing the issue. So over time you quit touching as much, because it might lead to that awkward moment. It wears on you. You miss the contact, question your manhood, and wonder if you're still attractive. You consider having an affair, but you know that's just a temporary fix that brings larger problems. So you learn to live with it and watch this wall being built, brick by brick, between you."

What's surprising is that more men in Aaron's situation aren't considering divorce or adultery. While we heard from a few guys who went this route, most intend to remain true. Whether because of children, finances, moral standards, or a simple aversion to change, they've resigned themselves to living platonically instead of passionately. But, according to Dr. Stein, the worst thing you can do is nothing. Living like this will hurt you not only emotionally, but also physically. Research shows that a lack of sex may compromise health and even shortens life. One study found that 45- to 59-year-old men having sex twice a week had a 68 percent lower death rate than those having sex once a month or less. Another study found that college students having sex at least once a week had enhanced immune systems compared with those who weren't as sexually active.

"The bottom line is that sex is just as health-promoting as vitamins, exercise, and a balanced diet," says Dr. Stein. "What we have here is not just a marital issue, but a significant public-health concern."

FROM GRIDLOCK TO SEX DRIVE

Some couples can mutually agree that sex is low priority and still enjoy a long, happy, fulfilling relationship. But they're in the minority. Most couples need regular sex not only to remain intimate, but even to stay civil to one other. If you and your partner are at sexual odds,

Predict Your Sexual Destiny

One of the most common complaints among married men is that sex with their mates used to be great, but now it's mundane and infrequent. "If I'd only known then what I know now . . . ," goes the lament. Based on the hundreds of reader letters we received, here are six warning signs to look for during courtship or in the early years of marriage. Spotting even one could mean you're heading for sexlessness.

Incredible premarital sex. The cruel truth is that the hotter the sex is before marriage, the more likely you'll be disappointed with it afterward. The tedium of living together year after year naturally saps desire; it's just impossible to remain as attracted to one another. But memories of those wild nights will persist, and the comparisons can spark blame and bitterness.

Faking orgasm. If she's not enjoying sex when it's new, it's doubtful she'll love it any more after it gets old. To tell whether she's really having a good time, listen. If she screams, she's faking. When climaxing, it's nearly impossible to exhale. The female orgasm is not an explosion; it's an implosion. She'll draw her breath, tighten her muscles, then give way to the flow of goodness spreading up her chest and down her legs. Afterward, she might sigh, pant, or moan. But scream? Never.

She wants to have lots of kids. Nothing changes a woman's sexuality like pregnancy and childbirth. Not only are there a host of physical and

here's a multistep program, crafted with the help of our experts, for breaking the gridlock and restoring intimacy to your relationship.

VIEW IT AS A "COUPLE PROBLEM." From this day forth, vow to stop the finger-pointing. This isn't her fault or your fault. This is a problem the two of you share. As Barry McCarthy, Ph.D., a certified sex therapist, points out in his book *Rekindling Desire*, the solution is to start working together. This simple shift in mindset can make a major difference.

emotional problems that can happen, such as loss of vaginal sensation and poor body image, but the demands of being a mother are also a major energy sapper. Sex will drop precipitously on her to-do list.

She can't have any kids. Nothing puts more strain on a relationship than fertility problems. Being poked and prodded by doctors and making love according to a schedule make sex seem mechanical. And if a baby doesn't result, the subsequent blame can be poisonous to a relationship.

Sexual scars from childhood. If your wife-to-be has a traumatic sexual experience in her past, it could become a roadblock to intimacy in your relationship. The chances of this happening are greater if she's never received psychological treatment for it. That demure, hesitant lover you find so challenging now may never open up.

She stops watching you walk away. A *Men's Health* reader who divorced his wife because of intimacy problems suggests this simple test: "When you're out to dinner and you leave the table to go to the bathroom, watch to see if her eyes follow you. When you have a healthy sex life and your lover gets up to walk away, you watch them leave. You look at them as they move. You enjoy the view. It's what lust makes you do. My ex stopped watching me walk away. The lust, the fire, the passion wasn't there. And because it wasn't there, now neither am I."

ELIMINATE POSSIBLE PHYSICAL CAUSES OF LOW DESIRE. There may be a very straightforward biological reason why your partner is disinterested in sex. Becoming a mother, for example, can dramatically affect a woman's sexuality, either by altering her physically or draining her mentally. Poor body image, stress, fatigue, surgical complications, menopause, and even the side effects of some drugs (especially antidepressants) can all have a negative impact. Likewise, a man's loss of desire can stem from naturally declining testosterone levels (see

"Check Your Testosterone" on page 192), performance anxiety, low-grade exhaustion, alcoholism, job stress, or certain medications. It's important to consider, and deal with, all of these possible causes by consulting a physician first.

CALL A HOOTCHY-KOOTCHY HIATUS. If the problem turns out to be psychological rather than physical, institute a temporary ban on intercourse. It doesn't matter if you've been getting laid less than fuchsia linoleum. By agreeing to have no nooky for a specified period, you'll be taking the heat off whoever is feeling pressured in the relationship. This usually helps that partner relax enough to open up. It'll also show the one with itchy fingers that there are other ways to express affection.

Try this: Lie on the bed, close your eyes, and ask your partner to touch and massage various parts of your body (genitals are off-limits). Focus on the sensations. Then do the same for her. McCarthy says this teaches you to separate pleasure from performance. Or here's another trick from the book *Supersex:* To stop trying to guess when your partner is in the mood, give her a refrigerator magnet. Tell her to move it up or down on the fridge to indicate her level of desire. This will keep you from initiating sex at the wrong time and triggering an argument.

MAKE A DATE FOR SEX. As your intercourse ban winds down, arrange for a special evening, just like when you were dating. Dr. Stein calls it "setting the table for sex." Reserve a babysitter, leave provocative notes for one another, visualize the two of you having the perfect romantic evening. One thing you shouldn't do, though, is go out for a big dinner. Save your blood supply for arousing your genitals instead of digesting the lamb chops. "Most couples don't spend any time planning for intimacy," says Dr. Stein, "but sex is all about expectation."

JUST DO IT. No doubt, the two of you will have a wonderful time on your "date." It'll be like old times, and you'll agree you should do this more often. To make sure you follow through, schedule sex as you would any other appointment, going as far as to write it on your calendar. It may sound cold, but new research shows that desire doesn't necessarily precede arousal. "My clients often say, 'I wasn't in the mood when we started, but once we got into it, I really enjoyed it,' " says Weiner Davis. "Some people rarely or never find themselves fantasizing about sex or feeling sexual urges, but when they're open to becoming sexual, they find the stimulation pleasurable, and they become aroused. Sometimes the hardest part of running is putting on your shoes. So just do it."

STAY CONNECTED BETWEEN "APPOINTMENTS." To keep a relationship vibrant, you have to communicate. It sounds obvious, but many couples don't do it. "With some couples, there's very little interaction," says Weiner Davis. "They may eat dinner together, but they're probably not talking much, and afterward they probably pursue separate activities. Then they're surprised they've grown apart and aren't having sex." You don't have to be each other's best friend or soul mate. All it takes, she says, is 15 minutes of daily check-in. It doesn't even matter what you talk about; what's important is that you're talking, touching, and expressing everyday concern and affection. "This sort of daily connection and friendship," she says, "is the foundation for keeping sexuality alive."

MAKE SEX PRIORITY ONE. Now that you know that lack of sex can depress your immune system and even shorten your life, what more incentive do you need to make it a priority? "Sex is more important than your career and even your kids," says Dr. Stein. "Your career will change, and your children will grow up and leave home, but in the end there will be the two of you." Plus, the longer you abstain from sex, the harder it is to get back in the saddle. Legendary sex therapists Masters and Johnson found that if women don't make love for long periods, it becomes harder for them to have an orgasm. Likewise, men who abstain often develop arousal problems or performance anxiety.

BEAT BEDROOM BOREDOM. Most of us enjoy a smorgasbord of va-

Check Your Testosterone

Testosterone is the juice of manhood. It helps make muscle and grow hair, and it contributes to aggressiveness and cravings for sex. But the power of this essential hormone begins to deteriorate after age 24. A significant loss of interest in sex may mean your tank is low.

"Testosterone is the hormone of desire," explains Dr. Daniel Stein, M.D., medical director of the Foundation for Intimacy, in Tampa, Florida. "In men, there is an inevitable decline with age that causes them to lose interest and ability. So what's wrong may be as simple as low testosterone. If your insulin were too low, you'd have diabetes, and you'd get it treated. For the overwhelming majority of men who lose desire, the problem isn't in their heads; it's in their hormones."

Testosterone can be measured two ways: by either an over-the-counter saliva test or a blood test. The latter is more accurate. Have your doctor draw the blood, and make sure he tells the lab to measure both free and bound testosterone. "Every man over age 35 should have this done," says Dr. Stein. "If nothing else, it provides a baseline for future comparison." Normal testosterone levels are between 800 and 1,200. If yours is under 500, Dr. Stein says you should consider testosterone replacement. This can be done through injections, a rub-on gel, or a patch.

According to a national survey, four million to five million American men have below-normal testosterone levels, and 5 percent are receiving replacement therapy. This type of treatment does entail some health risks, though, namely a possible link to prostate cancer. (A federal task force is expected to make more specific recommendations soon.)

In the meantime, to safeguard your testosterone level, you may want to consider taking a daily herbal supplement called Alzre. According to Dr. Stein, it seems to enhance desire, erection strength, and sexual performance. One thing you shouldn't put much hope in, though, is Viagra. "It has no effect on desire," he says, "and a lot of men don't realize that."

riety in every aspect of our lives except one: sex. It's tough enough that we're limited to one partner, but must we also limit ourselves to one night of the week, one side of the bed, one primary position? No wonder so many marriages are becoming sexless. Dr. Stein, the author of *Passionate Sex*, recommends two new devices that don't carry the same seedy rep as sex toys and actually have a scientific basis:

1. Liberator shapes. These are specially designed portable cushions (the Wedge, Ramp, Stage, and Cube) that help couples explore new positions. "They enhance the contact between the penis and the most sensitive spots of a woman's anatomy," he explains. "They're probably the most significant breakthrough in sexual health that I've seen in the past decade." They cost $65 to $180 and can be found at liberatorshapes.com.

2. GyneFlex vaginal exerciser. This plastic device, which looks like a wishbone, fits into the vagina. By using her pelvic muscles to squeeze its arms together, a woman can gradually increase her sexual responsiveness and orgasmic ability. "It's a Bowflex for the forgotten muscles," says Dr. Stein. "By doing three sets of 20 repetitions every other day for 8 weeks, a woman can revolutionize her sexual response regardless of age." And those tighter muscles feel pretty good for the guy, too. You'll pay about $40 for these toys; check out gyneflex.com.

IF ALL ELSE FAILS, SEE A THERAPIST. Consult the yellow pages for a certified sex therapist in your area, or visit the Web site of the American Association of Sex Educators, Counselors, and Therapists (aasect.org) for a directory. If one of you is too self-conscious to meet with a therapist in person, Weiner Davis runs the Divorce Busting Center (divorcebusting.com), which offers phone consultations with trained relationship coaches. Sessions cost $120 for 45 to 50 minutes. Call (800) 664-2435 or (815) 337-8000 for information and appointments.

"I've been married for 28 years," adds Dr. Holstein, the director of women's health at Canyon Ranch Resort in Tucson. "Like everyone else, my husband and I go through periods when we're not feeding our sexual energy. After a while I'll find myself getting irritable, then all of a sudden we'll come back together, and all is right with the world again. Folks don't recognize soon enough when they're losing that energy. It can happen in days. Then, of course, the longer you go, this Grand Canyon develops between the two of you, and you don't know how to cross it. We *need* that spark of connecting. You can do it with a glance, a kiss, or a touch. It's the kind of attention that needs to become habitual in a relationship."

"If we don't take steps to prevent sexlessness," concludes Dr. Stein, "we'll all end up sexless. It's that common."

Chick Flicks

A Conversation with Candida Royalle

In the world of adult entertainment, Candida Royalle fills a unique—and, some would say, vital—niche. Since 1984, Royalle has helmed Femme Productions, producing, writing, and directing porn for women. (Or, as Royalle calls her films, "Sensually Explicit Erotica from a Woman's Point of View for Couples to Share.") Her films are defined not so much by what they include—literal-minded folks would still consider her work hard-core porn—as by what they don't. In her movies, there are few, if any, close-ups of genitals. There are no shots of men ejaculating on women's faces, the colloquially known "money shots." The actors and actresses are attractive but not necessarily silicon-inflated nymphs. And there is always a sense that the couples respect each other's bodies and feelings.

Since its inception, Femme has proved that women buy porn, too. For themselves. That's good news for any man who keeps his Jenna Jameson videos tucked away, fearing his girlfriend or wife would disapprove. Your woman may be open to using porn (and other sexual aids, like vibrators) to heighten your sex life, Royalle says. The trick is deciding what to select and when and how to introduce it.

When porn is introduced into a couple's sex life, it's usually men doing the introducing, right?

I think it's wrong to assume that men like porn and women don't. In recent years, I've heard stories where women wanted to watch and their men didn't—the guy was bothered by it. There's a lot more acceptance. Especially with young women who haven't been brought up in an anti-pornography environment.

Also, there's been a mainstreaming of porn. I think a tide turned with the Larry Flynt movie with Woody Harrelson, and with *Boogie Nights*. When porn started getting plotlines, in the mid '70s, it was almost fashionably risqué to go to theaters and see it. That died off, but I feel like it's happening again. People are curious and want to look again. When I started Femme, there were about 100 new releases a year. Now there are 10,000. That tells you something about the marketplace. And it's not just all men.

That said, women in our culture still need permission to explore our sexuality. We're still indoctrinated to think we're not visual; we're uncomfortable with certain types of sex and sex play. As women receive more permission, we're reaching out and realizing we like things we never realized we liked. The good girl/bad girl stigma is out there, but we're putting a dent in it.

Let's imagine a scenario where a man wants to watch porn with his wife or girlfriend, but she resists. Should that guy never try to get his woman to watch porn with him?
I don't think men should assume their women should like adult entertainment. No one should have to like anything.

But she might really not be considering the range of adult entertainment. A lot of men and women have thanked me because they didn't think they liked it until they discovered my work. I think for most people, "porn" conjures a certain formulaic idea: videos with hardcore sex and certain kinds of scenes, angles, and sex acts. They imagine something that lacks real feeling or creativity. Unfortunately, a lot of porn is like that.

Anyone who thinks all adult movies are that way, though, hasn't viewed a wide enough variety of porn or adult movies. They need to be more open-minded. If someone is completely uncomfortable with explicit sex, they can find close-to-adult movies—very sexy movies that aren't explicit. Or they can find softer cable versions of most adult movies out there. It's definitely something worth exploring.

Any suggestions on how the man might broach the subject?

He might point out the ways adult movies can enhance and enrich a relationship. They open people up to new ideas, fantasies, things they'd like to try. They help open up the discussion. It's still difficult for people to ask for what they want or need. Especially women. If they see something they'd like to try, it's easier to refer to something on-screen than to point to yourself. Instead of saying, "I'd really like it if you did A, B, and C," you could turn to your partner and say, "Ever think of doing that?"

Adult entertainment is also a good way to jump-start the mood for a two-career couple or even with a one-career couple, where you're at home and exhausted at the end of the day. And it can be informative and educational, showing how women like to be pleased.

We can imagine a man making these points and the woman scoffing at him.

That's the reason why I try to put accurate and positive depictions of sex in my movies. I used to get so annoyed with movies that show women in the throes of ecstasy because guys were coming on their faces. I mean, it's good to get into kinky sex every once in a while, but it's also good to know techniques for how to get a woman off. Really only about 30 percent of women can have a vaginal orgasm. Many need direct clitoral stimulation; many need to use a vibrator. It would be useful to show them how.

In one of my early movies, I had one couple portraying a married couple. And I said to the actor, "After you've had intercourse for a while, I want you to pull out, before you come, go down on the woman and let her have her orgasm, than go back to intercourse." You'd think most men would know that going down on a woman is really effective, but some don't know how.

Another thing I like to show is ample foreplay and afterplay. These are things they can observe and learn from.

If you have a movie that's not accurate, it's one thing if a guy understands this is fantasy, but it's not good sex education. Unfortunately, it's still some of the only sex ed people get.

What are some things people see in porn that they shouldn't do?

I'm troubled by the over portrayal of anal sex. It can be exciting, but when you have so much of it in these films, there's a pressure to perform it. It's something that in moderation can be fun, but it's overdone. I think it's especially dangerous when you see a man going from anus to vagina. That's a no-no. That's the quickest way for infection.

Also, if you depict people getting into bondage play or S&M, it's important to show it as totally consensual—that it's agreed upon and negotiated, not forced.

What about the argument that women think their partners would rather be with the woman on the screen?

This is a very common belief women have and it makes them very insecure. First and foremost, you have to make your partner believe that she is the one you want—that she is, in your eyes, the sexiest, most beautiful woman in the world. Without that, she'll never be comfortable. She's always going to think you would prefer the women on-screen and don't find her sexy enough.

I use myself as an example. I never had a problem viewing porn with men who make me feel appreciated and beautiful. But I once had a lover who made me feel I wasn't very sexy, even though he protested. And I had no desire to watch anything with him. It made me feel insecure. Me!

So let's assume a couple has decided to watch porn together. Both parties are comfortable with the idea. How would you suggest they find something they will both like?

When people say, "There are so many. How do I find the best?" I say find the director that you like. You can always go by the director. Distributors will have a wide range of movies, everything from amateur to really well-done stuff. But the director will always be the same. You can always tell the difference between a Seymour Butts movie and a Candida Royalle movie.

If you go shopping together, look for women-friendly video stores. There's Babes in Toyland and Eve's Garden in New York, Good Vibrations in San Francisco, Hustler Hollywood in L.A., Grand Opening! in L.A. and Cambridge, Massachusetts. There are women there who will give you suggestions. And there are a growing number of women-friendly Web sites.

What would you look for when you're there?

In general, don't just look for sexy box covers at the adult video shop. Some videos, when you take them home, you discover there's been more time spent on the box than on what's inside. There are books available that talk about what movies would be enjoyed by women or men. You're probably talking more about men introducing to women. Good Vibrations has a book that lists movies that are more women-friendly.

If you're not sure or she's not sure how she'll feel, start with the nonexplicit versions of adult movies—these softer "cable" versions are usually available if you ask for them. Look for something that isn't formulaic. Be open. Also, when a woman feels like the guy is trying to push it on her, there will be resistance. And be sensitive to why she's resistant. Some women have been brought up with antipornography indoctrination. Some have suffered sexual abuse that can make it painful to look at sexually explicit material. You have to be sensitive to these things.

Some guys reading this are going to think your style of filmmaking, or anything softer than the porn they are used to, may not be enough for them. What would you say to the guys who like the classic stuff.
I'd say equal time, maybe. He needs to be more open and not judgmental. Maybe, by showing he's open to viewing something exciting to her, maybe he can get her to share work he prefers.

It's really important to remain open. Men have to remember that women have been brought up with a lot of repressive ideas. Men are the ones who will have to be more patient, particularly if you want her to view anything with you.

Let's turn out attention to another sex tool: the vibrator. You've helped develop some, I understand.
I've created a line of toys called Natural Contours, and sales have been great. There's no doubt women want their sex toys.

Let's say you're at the adult video store, ready to buy a movie, and your girlfriend or wife slips a vibrator into your shopping basket. How should men approach this twist?
Men shouldn't feel like they are being replaced and shouldn't give women a hard time about this. A man who is secure with his sexuality is going to be open to anything that brings her more pleasure. To act like "Oh, you don't need me" is ridiculous. She's not trying to push him away. When my man uses a toy on me, I think that turns me on even more. In the end, the fact is that some women require a vibrator to get off. If that's the case, I think it would be foolish not to bring it into bed with you.

QUICKIES

STAY HAPPY TOGETHER

An old-time baseball writer once told us the secret to his happy 40-year marriage: road trips. A little space can make the marriage stronger, says David H. Olson, Ph.D., author of *Empowering Couples*. The reunions can rock, too. Here are some simple steps to keep your wedded state blissful.

Enter That Mountain-Bike Race

Couples who play sports together reduce their stress and feel closer in their relationship, says Bonnie Eaker Weil, Ph.D., a couples therapist in New York City and author of *Make Up, Don't Break Up*. The wilder the better: "The adrenaline rush will be channeled into your romance."

Time-Travel

Pull out the photo album or home movies . . . like the ones from way back when you were at your youngest, supplest, and most attractive. "It turns you on to each other again," says Weil.

Make Your Organs Bigger

Your brains, that is. "Try gardening, taking a course, attending a lecture, or taking up a musical instrument together," suggests Weil. You'll boost your compatibility as you share enthusiasm.

HER ULTIMATE WEAPON:
THE NO-SEX SHIELD

A recent Harris Interactive survey found that 22 percent of women withhold sex as punishment after an argument—a number that seems suspiciously low. (This survey, sponsored by Adam & Eve, an adult-products company, said 12 percent of men do the same.) Robert

Glover, Ph.D., author of *No More Mr. Nice Guy: A Proven Plan for Getting What You Want in Love, Sex and Life,* suggests this strategy for a resumption of talks.

Write a Note
Keep it short and simple: You love her, and you're available to talk when she's ready. Send only one—a repeat makes you look needy and weak, which you're not.

Have Guy Time
"A man should go to work, hang out with his buddies, mow the lawn, play with the dog," says Glover. "He can take care of his own sexual urges in private."

Be Patient
Let her cool off. "She has eventually returned every other time you've had a fight—she probably will this time, too," says Glover. "If you're patient, the payoff will be worth the wait."

THE MOAN ZONE: ORAL-SEX TIPS FROM THE MOUTHS OF BABES

In her view (we asked), a man's most reliable bedroom body part is his tongue. Hey, whatever works—a mind-blowing orgasm for her leads to reciprocal behavior, pressure-free sex, and more fun for everyone.

To begin, go slowly. "Anticipation is everything," says Tracey Cox, author of *Supersex.* "Work slowly down her body, and kiss, nibble, and lick every inch of skin you encounter on your way south." The key is to have her squirmingly aroused before you reach your target. Keep in mind: Her instrument is a violin (unlike your brassy, extendable trombone), sensitive to the slightest variations in tone and pressure. Stroke with care.

Men Ask—And the Women Answer . . .
• How well do you have to know a man before you feel okay about his going downstairs?

"We'd have to be fairly intimate: a few dates, a few conversations about personal lives, some level of trust and respect," says Elizabeth, 28, a journalist.

"I don't need to know a man all that well. Chemistry and attraction make me comfortable," says Emily, 29, an event coordinator.

• Should a man signal what he wants to do?
"All couples have their own lingo, but I don't think a man always needs to indicate his move. It's sexier when he just takes control and eases himself down there," says Elizabeth.

"If it's a new relationship, he should slowly kiss all the way down my body; I'll get the hint. If I'm into it, I'll let him know by tilting my pelvis up. If it's a long-term relationship, it's fun to talk dirty and be blunt," says Marie, 28, a real-estate agent.

• What makes a man bad at oral sex?
"If he doesn't appear to be enjoying himself, then I can't let myself enjoy him, either," says Elizabeth.

"Changing the pressure or position too much. Variety is great in the beginning, but when I get close, keep it steady," says Marie.

"I once had oral sex with a human Electrolux—there was so much suction that it was painful. And any involvement of the teeth is definitely bad," says Lucia, 31, an architect.

MAKE IT PERSONAL: A BETTER VALENTINE

Dinner and roses? Uninspired. "There's nothing very special about being just like every other woman on February 14," says Michael Webb, author of *The RoMANtic's Guide*. Show that you put some thought into the day. With these:

Her Favorite Take-Out Food for Dinner
You care enough to have remembered. Use good plates.

Romantic DVDs Bundled into a Personal Boxed Set
Include movies you've seen together, or classics; it's creative and thoughtful.

A Fun, Decadent Dessert

Try this fondue from Colin Cowie, author of *Dinner after Dark*: Melt any chocolate (even Hershey bars) in a saucepan, mix in heavy cream, and dip strawberries, biscotti, or her favorite cookies.

A Foot Massage Using a Fragrant Oil

You can take it from here, right?

KNIGHT MOVES

Women love heroes. Use a little modern-day chivalry to help you land damsels without distress.

It must have been easier to feel heroic in ye olden days: Castles, steeds, and enchanted swords are better props than Toyotas and tract houses. But she'll willingly yield to your Sir Lance-a-lot fantasies if she can see the gleam in your armor: polite, thoughtful, romantic gestures delivered with a certain throwback boldness—not just on Valentine's Day, but anytime. (In fact, the more unexpected the better.) It's admirable to perform these actions in a spirit of noble altruism. But let's get real: These heroic deeds lead to good things for everyone—dates for single guys, increased devotion from girlfriends and wives, and more one-eyed-dragon slaying all around. Read on to see what the experts and Guineveres of 2003 told us.

"Women have always been drawn to protective, strong, brave men," says Ava Cadell, Ph.D., author of *12 Steps to Everlasting Love*. "Heroic deeds make women feel wanted, secure, and turned on." That gut feeling may be a holdover from caveman days. Today's hero can win her favor with simple kindness.

Rescue Her from a Party Bore

Watch for fidgeting or a wandering gaze, then slide in for the save. "If a man knows instinctively when a woman is experiencing this, she'll feel like he can read her mind," says Cadell.

Maintain Her Castle While She's Away

Volunteering to house-sit her place is an intimate act, according to Dr. Freud. And if you can fix that faucet and shop for the welcome-home meal, even better. "Heroic without being macho. It's compassionate and generous, and says you know what's important to her," says Cadell.

Scrape Her Windshield While She Sleeps

"Women love it when men take initiative in a thoughtful way," says Celeste Gertsen, Ph.D., a clinical psychologist whose research shows that heroic traits like courage, devotion, discipline, and an ability to overcome obstacles rank high with women.

Give Your First-Class Ticket to a Woman Who's Traveling Alone with a Baby

This sort of selfless act plays well to female witnesses. "Any kindness to children, the elderly, or animals will elevate an ordinary guy to heroic status," says Lisa Daily, author of *Stop Getting Dumped!* "The same traits that make you help an old woman cross the street will also make you chase down an ice-cream truck when I'm pregnant."

The Ladies Say . . .

"It was really late at night and I was driving. My boyfriend knew I was on the road and probably sleepy, so he called to make sure I was okay. He kept me company—and awake—until I was almost there," says Tonya, 22, a student.

"A hero is the same now as he was in the time of white horses and castles. He is strong, he protects, he makes you feel cherished and singled out. The modern part of the equation is that he does all these things but lets you pretend not to need them in front of the rest of the world," says Andrea, 28, a gallery owner.

"For me, it's less about individual gestures and more about overall character. A hero sees his heroine; he can get inside her [Yeah!—eds.] and do the big and small things to make her feel special," says Blaire, 26, an ad executive.

ASK THE GIRL
NEXT DOOR
The honest truth about women
from our lovely neighbor

What Do You Think?
What does "I think we should see other people" really mean?

—TOM B., NEW HAVEN, CONNECTICUT

It means your girlfriend is pretty sure you're not "the one," so she wants to resume her search for him ASAP but wouldn't mind your company while she's looking. Same as when you use that line.

Hard and Fast Rules
Do women prefer slow sex?   —MATTHEW D., WESTPORT, CONNECTICUT

I'm glad you asked, because I've had more than one friend complain to me that her too-sensitive boyfriend never grabs her, bends her over something sturdy, and gives it to her like he means it. When you're in a loving, trusting relationship, a little playful aggression can be a major turn-on. So even though there are those times when long, slow, gentle lovemaking is exactly what we want, there are a lot of other nights when fast, hard, and happenin' feels even better.

Preggers Patrol
My wife recently became pregnant. I really want to be there for her. Can you give me any advice?   —CRAIG, BRATTLEBORO, VERMONT

I checked with a pregnant friend who just had her first ultrasound (and is freaking out because her fetus looks like a chipmunk) and another who gave birth to a baby boy 2 months ago. They both agree that you should read the same pregnancy and childbirth books your wife is reading. That way you'll know almost as much about what her body is going through as she does. Offering to do "anything" to help when she's experiencing wild mood swings or wicked back pain also would be in-credibly sweet—just don't claim to know exactly what would be best for her or she'll bite your head off. Speaking of which, being verbally decapitated is something you should prepare yourself for anyway. The most wonderful, generous thing you could possibly do for your wife, says my preggo friend, is to allow her to bite without your biting back. That's love.

She's Wearing His Underwear

What are some of the signs that a woman is cheating on her hus-band or boyfriend?   —ANONYMOUS

Did you see the movie *Unfaithful?* If not, rent the DVD—it'll make all of your past failed relationships look like a walk in the park. The way-ward wife, played by Diane Lane, shows all the classic signs.

If she's two-timing you, a woman will start turning down your in-vitations, claiming she's too busy with friends, hair appointments, or work to spend time with you. She'll be less talkative and more dis-tracted but won't have a convincing explanation when you ask her why. She'll stop initiating sex—and when you try, she'll act uncomfortable and hesitant. She may also be spending a suspicious amount of time on her cell phone out of earshot, or sending e-mails late at night. When you call her, she'll sound vaguely disappointed that it's you. Look out for new dresses, shoes, and lingerie that you never see her wear. Is she glowing and happy and giggly, yet not directing any of that positive energy toward you? Then the source of that glow might be another man.

For more honest answers about women, look for Ask the Men's Health *Girl Next Door wherever books are sold.*

6

THE NEXT LEVEL

Everyone gets stuck in a rut sometimes. Think Andre Agassi. John Travolta. Ozzy Osbourne. Each one, a great in his field. Each one, a man who succumbed to the pressures of success. Each one, revived by a comeback.

The same pattern is evident in relationships—even the great ones. Do it the same way, day in, day out, and your sex life is bound to stall. Fortunately, a comeback is just a matter of breaking bad habits, re-tapping your talents, and maybe learning a new trick or two. When you hit a lull, you have a choice: Do nothing, or do it different.

We say do it different. The following pages will show you how to change things up and take them to the next level. Get ready for *your* comeback.

15 Things She Doesn't Want to Hear in Bed

Talk the Talk, Watch Her Walk   BY ALIX STRAUSS

1. "Do you want to take a shower first?"

2. Chris Berman.

3. "He shoots, he scores," or any other sort of sports metaphor.

4. Whitesnake singing "Is This Love," Poison singing "Every Rose Has Its Thorn," and the remaining 12 songs on your '80s power-ballads compilation disc.

5. **Your roommate watching *Girls Gone Wild Doggy Style* on the other side of the wall.**

6. [Gulp] "I don't really keep track. Maybe 35 . . . you know, give or take a few . . . or five."

7. Any comments whatsoever about her intimate grooming habits.

8. "Are those real?"

9. "Julie . . . from the gym" on your machine, saying she had "an ab fab time" at couples' yoga yesterday.

10. **The silent roar of your leopard-print silk sheets.**

11. "Let me slip in halfway, and then I'll use a condom." (Yes, there really are men who say stuff like this.)

12. Comments about her sheets. It scares her when you know thread counts.

13. "Do you want to keep going?"

14. "I'm ready for a cold one."

15. **"Herpes."**

Talk to Her!

Eight simple statements that are worth a thousand dirty pictures

BY LISA JONES

THE FIRST TIME I GOT NAKED WITH BEN, somewhere between peeling off my shirt and unzipping my jeans, he whispered, "You're all soft and shit."

It looks pathetic in print, but at the time, my knees turned to pudding. It helped that his voice was steady and soft, his lips close to my ear. That his words were an endearing mix of tender and guy. That he said it at the moment his hands were securely wrapped around the small of my back and his bare chest was pressed against mine: the moment when I'll believe anything a man tells me.

Later, as we lay facing each other, listening to John Mayer, Ben locked his brown eyes with mine, leaned in, and said, "You do good work."

"Your Body Is a Wonderland" played, and I swallowed a gag. I felt like a whore, and when he finally fell asleep, I dressed in the dark and went home.

Ben was a good guy—he did good work, too, while it lasted. He just didn't understand the power that his words, no matter how innocent, could have on a naked woman. How in five simple whispered words, a man can set a woman throbbing. How in 3 seconds and four syllables he can so crushingly disappoint. How easy it is to do both without realizing it.

Ben's tongue gaffe doesn't even rank among the top three worst things a man has ever said to me in bed. That list: "This was a mistake." (Which it was, but still.) "I know when you're faking." (Which I wasn't.) "Thank you." (Again, the whore thing.)

The list of best things is, sadly, more difficult to compile. It's understandable, I suppose—we never tell you what we like to hear in bed. Let's assume you've said enough of the right words so far, since she's already gotten semi-naked. Now follow these guidelines and you'll become the elusive man she's longing for: the man with a well-trained tongue.

"IT'S OKAY FOR US TO GO SLOW"

Say it and mean it. Especially when you're first rubbing skin with a new woman and it's not yet clear whether you'll actually have sex tonight or everything but. Or when you're first getting back together with an ex. Or when you're about to have sex with her for the first time since she gave birth. It builds trust and reassures a woman that you care more about her than about the sex. Also, it often leads to the reverse-psychology phenomenon: She'll want to jump you by the time you finish the sentence. Or maybe that's just me.

"THIS HEART-SHAPED FRECKLE ON YOUR RIGHT INNER THIGH IS SO BEAUTIFUL"

Compliments are always good. Except when they're generic. Then she thinks you've said the same thing to 47 other women. Focus on unique details—the way her lips curl or her eyes crinkle. The more special you make her feel, the more aroused she gets. She wants to hear words that imply she's attractive, appreciated, loved—or at least liked. Compliments after sex are good, too. (Just beware of "You do good work.") "Women feel disheveled after sex—without makeup, hair all messy," says Ava Cadell, Ph.D., author of *Stock Market Orgasm*. "If a man tells a woman he loves the way she looks after sex, that's a bonus point."

"YOU"

Say it often. "You" is the hottest word you can say to a woman in bed. "You make me feel so good" instead of "That feels so good." Subtle modification, but big difference in sentiment. "'You' is sexy because you're referring to her as opposed to the act of sex," says Daylle Deanna Schwartz, a psychotherapist and author of *How to Please a Woman in and out of Bed*. "It's very personal, and women love that."

"YOU KISS GREAT FOR A VIRGIN, BRITNEY."

A woman needs feedback to know she's turning you on. "Oh, yeah. You feel so good. Holy f*#&%@g G—." You're shooting from the frontal lobes here, and verbal cues of any kind work. Even grunting. It indicates that you really liked it when she grabbed your ass, but didn't care for the sucking of toes. Need inspiration to get vocal? "Women are much more likely to give longer and more enthusiastic oral sex when men give them a response," says Schwartz. When you drift into radio silence, she starts wondering, "Is this doing anything for him? Should I stop? Does my face look fat?" All that thinking keeps her from, um, concentrating.

"I'M GOING TO TAKE THESE OFF"

Compare this with "Should I take these off?" Too many questions make sex seem clinical and cerebral, and women hate that. Also, women want the man to convey a sense of certainty. When he does, it creates an intimate space where she can feel safe to open up. Sometimes midthrust queries are necessary, in which case it's best to whisper urgently in her ear. A better time for questions is before or after sex, while you're holding her.

"YOU MAKE ME THINK DIRTY THOUGHTS"

Your last girlfriend liked you to swear like Missy Elliot. Your new girlfriend might, too. You just don't know yet: You've had only sweet, respectful, beginning-of-relationship sex. It's time for a dirty-talk litmus test—make a statement like the one above and see if she turns red. "Some women hate the 'c-word' but love the 'p-word,'" says David Copeland, coauthor of *How to Talk to Women*. "Some feel the opposite. Some dislike both. It's best to test a bit, rather than go for your deepest, kinkiest dirty talk right away." Be attuned to her response before you take it up a notch on the dirty scale. "Know that you are likely to offend a woman at some point," says Copeland. When this happens, revert immediately to PG-rated compliments, à la, "Did I mention that lovely freckle on your thigh?"

"I WANT TO MAKE YOU FEEL GOOD"

You want her to have an orgasm, and you want her to know it. But talking about it is one way to ensure it won't happen—it sometimes comes across as your being more concerned about your abilities than about how she feels. "Focus not on orgasm, but on giving her sexual pleasure," says Laura Berman, Ph.D., a clinical professor at Northwestern University and director of the Berman Center in Chicago. "It's more erotic." Swap in the words "feel good" and "pleasure" for "orgasm" in your vocabulary.

"NEXT TIME, I'M GOING TO TAKE YOU ON THE HOBBYHORSE"

Afterplay is just as important for building her arousal as foreplay, and it takes only a fraction of the time. "Create sexual anticipation by telling her what you're going to do to her next time," suggests Cadell. "It conveys that you care about her and want to satisfy her." And it lets her know she's still desirable to you, even after you've had your way with her.

Eternal Lovin'

Tantric sex—even without the sandals—could be the key
to better sex than you ever thought possible.

BY MATTHEW BARBOUR

ASK MOST MEN IN LONG-TERM RELATIONSHIPS if sex gets better with age, and all you'll hear are embarrassed coughs and a few chuckles.

But monogamous sex doesn't have to be mundane, says Val Sampson, author of *Tantra, The Art of Mind-Blowing Sex*. When it comes to sexual intercourse, most men treat their bodies as if they're old Honda Civics, Simpson says: little jalopies to get them from A to B—or, in this case, from insertion to orgasm—without breaking down. The trick is getting men to train their bodies for higher-octane performance.

"What men must realize is that you're born with the capacity of a Ferrari," Sampson says. "You can make the thrill of the journey, not arriving at the destination, the focus."

To find fifth gear, Simpson suggests an age-old tool: tantra

Tantra is essentially a series of 5000-year-old love teachings, aimed at building arousal very slowly so you both stay just below boiling point for as long as possible. Sampson says, "It's not ordinary sex being dragged out for hours. It's a completely different approach to making love, which enables men and women both to experience full-body orgasms, to be multiorgasmic, and share the best natural high there is."

HANG ON

"If there was a sex manual for the male body, the most important page would be the one explaining that orgasm is not the same as ejaculation," Sampson says. Tantra teaches men to experience a series of full-body orgasms rather than treating the normal six-second "genital sneeze" as the goal of sex. Here's how to get there.

SUCK AND BLOW. "Breathing is essential for delaying ejaculation," explains Sampson. As you approach heightened arousal, breathe in and out very deeply and slowly through your nose to slow down your heart and reduce the bloodflow to your penis, lessening the urge to ejaculate.

USE YOUR TONGUE. At the point where you feel you might be reaching your peak, press your tongue against the top of your palate. "By tensing muscles in your mouth, you move blood away from your groin, giving you a chance to recover," Sampson says. "Don't feel embarrassed, though—it's unlikely to cause too much of a distraction for your partner."

EMPTY YOUR TANK. Take to the bathroom before taking your partner. A full bladder will put more pressure on your prostate and pubococcygeus (PC) muscles, giving you less control.

SLOW IT DOWN, SON. "Your penis will feel much more sensual and even bigger if she's fully excited before you enter her," Sampson says. Focus on her entire body, kissing and massaging for at least 15 minutes until she's considering full-blown sex. "Try to alternate the way you touch her every 30 to 60 seconds, from touching to kissing, lighter or harder touches, to build the sexual charge."

HAND SOLO

To regularly achieve a real orgasm—without what Sampson calls "genital sneezing"—practice alone.

SLOW DOWN. "As kids, men rush masturbation, as they're afraid of getting caught," says Richard Craze, author of *Tantric Sexuality: A Beginner's Guide.* "Pretend you're focusing more on pleasing your imaginary partner to draw things out." As you near climax, stop and squeeze your PC muscles for 5 seconds.

LUBE UP. "For extra sensation, use a viscous oil rather than a lotion for lubrication," Craze advises. Choose a massage or baby oil, such as Johnson's Baby Oil.

GO DOWN. Instead of doing what most guys do, and focusing on the glans, concentrate on other parts of your manhood. "Rub farther down, or even massage your testicles while you do it to experience the full range of sensations," Craze says.

STEM THE FLOW. Use your index and middle fingers of one hand to press on your perineum, the stretch of skin that lies between your scrotum and your anus. In this way you can prevent the semen from leaving your prostate and entering your urethra before you ejaculate. "This little trick should stop the ejaculatory response without affecting your ability to experience orgasm," Craze claims.

MAX YOUR MUSCLES

Although there are no easy healthy ways to actually increase the size of your member, there are a few exercises you can do to help it work better.

GO PC. The pubococcygeus muscles, which control ejaculation, are the same ones we use when we hold in pee, giving us ample opportunity for practice. The next time you urinate, squeeze to stop the flow. Doing 20 rapid squeezes several times during the day will make these muscles stronger—and help you last longer. "When you get aroused, flex your PC muscles for 5 seconds and see what a difference it makes," Sampson suggests.

LIFT SOME WEIGHTS. To help strengthen your genital muscle control, try this little exercise. When erect, hang a wet face cloth over your penis, contract your muscles, and see how high you can lift it. "Aim for as many repetitions as possible in 30 seconds to improve control," advises Sampson.

FIRM UP. To encourage more blood to flow into the shaft of the penis, thereby giving you firmer erections, squeeze and hold the base of the shaft for 2 minutes, twice a day. "This increases the bloodflow in the spongelike tissues, making you firmer for longer," Sampson says.

SET THE SCENE

"You have to take control of the entire situation if you want to get the most out of it," explains Anne Johnson, author of *The Art of Tantric Sex*. Last-minute, rushed sex after a night of bar-hopping is not the way to go. Here's our sex-step guide to mixing the perfect brew of tantric passion.

CREATE YOUR SHRINE. Very few of us have the time to do much when we get back from the job, so simply clear a space of clutter—unplug the phone, and get rid of any take-home work or books that might distract you. "Create a calm atmosphere where you won't feel rushed or reminded of everyday responsibilities," says Johnson.

SHINE A LIGHT. But nothing too bright. Normal household bulbs send out a pallid yellow light that makes skin appear tinged with unflattering grey and white tones. "Either go for candles, which make it seem softer and warmer, or choose different colored bulbs," Johnson says.

In a recent U.S. study, men viewing women lit by green or blue light reported that their breasts not only looked larger but felt larger than they really were, while women also saw men's penises as larger. The same study revealed that red light hastened erection, for some unknown reason, while green light slowed it down.

SPIN SOME TUNES. "Fast music will cause your pulse to race, so go for something more relaxed, preferably below 60 beats per minute," says Johnson. So ditch the industrial German techno in place of your Ibiza chill-out if you want real results.

GET IN SYNC. "A perfect warm-up to sex is to lie together as close as possible almost without moving to coordinate your inhaling and exhaling," explains Craze. "This means that during sex you'll be working together as a team and become much more aware of what your partner is feeling." Try the spoon position, lying on your sides with one of you facing the back of the other, knees tucked in.

MAKE A STINK. Tantrics believe certain smells ignite sexual energy. "Scent detected by your olfactory nerve makes an immediate impact on the brain, while food and drink can take hours to enter the bloodstream," says Johnson.

As well as getting rid of any unpleasant smells by properly airing the room, try using massage oils, like Body Shop's Sensual Bath and Massage Oil, scented with musk, sandalwood and lavender, all shown in clinical trials to provoke arousal.

LOOK DEEP. "It might sound a bit New-Agey, but try sitting cross-legged opposite one another and silently gazing into each other's eyes for a full 2 minutes," explains Craze. This will help to reassure your partner that you've got her interests at heart, as well as heightening sexual tension before the big moment.

TANTRIC TRICKS

Now you've done the preparation, it's time to get to work. "With every position, get into the mindset of building up so you're close to the point of no return, then letting it subside," says Johnson. "The more times you repeat this sexual buildup, the longer you'll both last and the more sexual tension will mount, climbing towards a mind-blowing climax."

FAST-FORWARD NATION

Percentage of adults who have read a magazine or seen a movie/ video containing explicit sexual content in the past 7 days:

Source: *Barna Research Group Research Alert, 11/01/2002*

THRUST OF THE PHOENIX. Perhaps the most widely known tantric technique, this little winner can be used with any position. When you start thrusting, go in shallow, then one deep, then eight shallow, then one deep, working your way down to one shallow. "This has been known to give women who claim to never orgasm their first taste of the big 'O'," says Johnson. "Building slowly up to a big crescendo will have her willing to reach the climax."

THE TANTRA X. You sit cross-legged while your partner kneels over your lap, facing you with her calves under your knees. As you enter her, she uses her thigh muscles to lower herself up and down as slowly as possible. "Keep your bodies close together, using your hands to caress each other for maximum sensual contact," says Johnson.

SEXUAL SEE-SAW. With your partner lying on her back, slip a pillow beneath the small of her back so her pelvis is slightly raised. Then lift her feet up so that her legs are folded in, her knees almost resting on her breasts, the soles of her feet resting on your chest. "This will give your partner maximum penetration for perfect G-spot stimulation, while you'll have complete control over your thrusting to prolong your erection," Johnson says.

THE TANTRIC LOVE TRIANGLE. This is a sure-fire way to get your partner weeping with joy," explains Johnson. With your partner lying on her back, and you kneeling beside her at a right angle, insert your index and middle fingers inside her until the tips are pressing upward just beyond her pubic bone: prime G-spot territory. Then make a gentle "come here" movement with your fingers. Meanwhile, rest the palm of your other hand on her abdomen with your fingers pointing toward her clitoris. "The combination of G-spot stroking, pressure on her pubic area, and clitoris caressing will create a pleasure triple-whammy," says Johnson.

THE RUSTIC. Get your partner to lie on her back with her thighs pressed tightly together, and enter her with your thighs on the outside. "Because the vagina engulfs the penis completely, you'll both get maximum stimulation," she says.

THE BUFFET. While she's lying on the edge of a flat, sturdy surface, withdraw your penis completely from her and then penetrate her wholly in one shot. "Each time you withdraw she'll be desperate for more, increasing the sexual tension for both of you," says Johnson.

THE FINAL WORD

To paraphrase Woody Allen, even bad tantric sex is good sex. "Tantra gives men and women some techniques—sensual massage, eye contact, breathing routines—to help them slow down and get beyond goal-oriented sex," says sex therapist Gina Ogden. "Men manage to look beyond the ends of their penises while the urge to please a woman takes over. And women often take the initiative as a result."

Ogden believes tantric sex should not be seen as an all-or-nothing marathon session. "It's simply adding to your potential bedroom menu. Get yourself past the New Age jargon, ignore the creepy, pony-tailed hosts of every tantric how-to video, and what's left is the fundamentals of good sex: communication and variety."

Dirty Dozin'

They're weird, they're wild, and yes, sometimes they're wet.
We analyze your most common sex dreams—and explain
what's really going bump in the night.

BY LISA JONES

YOU'RE HAVING THE BEST SEX OF YOUR LIFE. With Jennifer Aniston. You're digging it. She's digging it. She's screaming your name. Cameron Diaz shows up. (Surprise, big guy!) But she just wants to cuddle and kiss, so you go back to Jennifer. It's smokin' hot. You're about to orgasm. But there's Cameron again—and she's scratching your back and nuzzling your neck. It's getting a little distracting. Suddenly your mom appears. And a parade of other people. You don't even recognize most of them. Who are they? Why are they in your bed? They seem to be having a party. They don't seem to notice or even mind that you're having sex. Your mom shakes your hand. You can't concentrate. You can't orgasm. You wake up.

Now, what the heck was that about?

This dream is bizarre, but it's not so unusual. Movie stars, pairs of women, and even moms are common characters in men's sex dreams. And the actual sex happening in your subconscious isn't always as enjoyable as it is interesting—fear and frustration are as common as pleasure for most dreamers. Still, even if your dreams sometimes seem as perverse as Michael Jackson's reality, research suggests you're normal. We've broken down some of the most common somnolent scenarios, and we'll venture some educated guesses as to what they're trying to tell you.

INTERRUPTED SEX

"Probably the most common sexual dream for men is interrupted sex," says Gayle Delaney, Ph.D., founding president of the Association for the Study of Dreams and author of *All about Dreams*. "You hardly ever have a sexual dream in which you come to orgasm. Usually things go wrong—it gets complicated."

Why can't you finish the job? It could be related to what's happening when you're awake. "These kinds of dreams can occur when you're not able to complete something in your life—maybe something work related," says Patricia Garfield, Ph.D., author of *Creative Dreaming*.

Or it could be that you're uptight about sex itself. Think about that frightening example in which your mom spoils your friendship with Jennifer A. "This dream happens most often when people are younger, in their 20s and 30s, when they're getting more comfortable with their own sexuality," says Delaney. "That's not what it means all the time, but it's generally how people work through their unfinished embarrassment about sexuality."

Amazing Dream Fact

Some blind people can see in their dreams, but whether their dreams feature visual imagery depends on when they lost their sight. People who are blind from birth seem to have dreams without visuals.

ANOTHER WOMAN

Don't feel guilty if you're cheating on your wife or girlfriend in your dreams. "Often, other-woman dreams are really about the woman you're with," says Delaney. Let's say you're standing facing your wife, but there's a beautiful, sexy woman standing behind her. You're trying to hug your wife so you can lean around and kiss the other woman. Does it mean you want to have an affair? A threesome? Sex on a subway during rush hour? Maybe none of the above. The sexy woman could really represent the things about your wife that turn you on.

And what if the Other Woman turns out to be, uh, the Other Species? "If you have a deviant dream about an animal, or an incestuous dream, don't worry. Think of the qualities the animal or family member represents to you," says Garfield.

FLIPPED ORIENTATION

Bob from accounting stops by for a visit in your dream. He kisses you. You wake up next to your girlfriend, confused and a little freaked out. What does it mean? You could want Bob. Perhaps the way his double chin wobbles when he says things like "maximize cross-brand efficiencies" just makes you feel all Siegfried and Roy. But don't switch teams and buy new shoes just yet.

"Heterosexuals have homosexual dreams all the time," says Kelly Bulkeley, Ph.D., a dream researcher in Berkeley, California. "It doesn't necessarily mean the dreamer is really gay. Those desires are simply a part of who we are, even if our primary orientation is heterosexual." Or such dreams may be a sign that you're spending a little too much time on you lately. "Having sex with someone too much like you can suggest you're turning your creative energies inward rather than outward," says Bulkeley.

Amazing Dream Fact

Dying in your dream doesn't mean you're really a goner. People have died in dreams and lived to report them.

CHEATING PARTNER

In your dream, your girlfriend of many years has sex with your best friend. You watch it happen. You wake up with a lingering feeling that she can't be trusted. Is it prophetic? Probably not. "Many times, people use sex in dreams as a metaphor for intimacy issues," says Delaney. "It could be that, in reality, you're neurotic because a woman left you for your best friend a long time ago. Your dream could just represent a fear." If this happens to you, ask yourself what qualities your buddy has and why your girlfriend might be attracted to them, says Delaney. Have you been getting lazy in the relationship? Is your girlfriend vulnerable to a new man?

Amazing Dream Fact

In men's dreams, male characters outnumber female characters two to one, whereas women dream equally about men and women.

WET DREAM

You had a wet dream. You're 35. What's the deal? The frequency of men's wet dreams peaks at age 18, says Delaney, but you can have one at any age. The reason: During REM sleep, when most dreaming occurs, there's increased bloodflow to the genitals. In men, this causes up to six erections a night.

Stimulation by rubbing or touching then usually brings on ejac-

PUT YOUR HANDS
WHERE SHE CAN'T SEE 'EM

Number of men who would agree to some patrol-car nooky with an unattractive woman cop if it would get them out of a ticket:

38%

Invade My Bed By Nicole Beland

My postcollege boyfriend—let's call him Seth—had no idea how bad he was in bed. When I remember his sweet but hopelessly ineffectual groping, licking, and grinding, the long nights of the winter of 1997 come vividly to mind. After he enjoyed an orgasm that made the veins on his arms pop like exposed electrical wiring, Seth would kiss me gratefully, flip onto his stomach, and pass out. I'd wait 10 minutes—an eternity, thanks to the ache of my neglected clitoris—and then slide out of bed to engage in a secret nightly ritual. I would lie down on a thick towel in the bathroom—that tile floor was freezing!—to service myself while Seth slept on. Near the end, I'd bite my lip to stifle involuntary, high-pitched cries (think Mariah Carey having her toes run over by an SUV). Seth never did catch me, which is too bad. Female masturbation has a way of making a guy ask questions.

I should have told Seth what he needed to know. But then, he never showed the slightest interest in how I was coming along—or not. I can forgive him for that, but I will never settle for it again.

Study up—and down. I want a man who's as interested in giving pleasure as he is in getting it; a man who's willing to ask the occasional soft-spoken question ("Would you like it better if I did this harder/softer, faster/slower?"); a man who logs extended minutes between my legs noticing how my body responds to different strokes, pressures, and thrusts (with tongue/fingers/penis). I want a man who understands that a woman has a lot to say about what turns her on, but needs to be encouraged to do so. How? Bring up the subject over a romantic dinner or while relaxing in the tub—situations that feel intimate and safe, but where there's no pressure to perform.

And the conversation will be a lot more interesting if you've shown due diligence in studying female physiology. I'd love to meet a man who has read one-tenth as many books and articles about female anatomy and

ulation, according to Ted McIlvenna, Ph.D., president of the Institute for Advanced Human Sexuality. "Only 15 percent of the time do men have an orgasm without touching or stimulation of the genitals," he says.

pleasure points as he has about sports and the stock market. I'll be the first to admit it: Bringing a woman to orgasm can be difficult, from one woman to the next and even one moment to the next. Consider yourself a precious find if you know one or two ways to put her over the top. Figure out two more and you'll be every woman's fantasy.

Lust me tender. Skills aside, I cherish bedmates who have mastered the combination of tenderness and raw lust that's crucial to keeping sex hot over months, years, and eventually decades. Just a few nights ago, I went out with a man who, the very first time he kissed me, grabbed me by the waist and pulled me against his body in a way that could only be described as aggressive. My thighs melted instantly, but his forward-ness made red flags fly: Was I sure I wanted to do this? A second later, his grip softened, and he leaned down and kissed me gently. There was no question that he was eager for the act, but he was also patient enough to approach me carefully and well. That's what amazing lovers are made of.

Use your (other) head. Which brings me to my last, most important de-sire: The man I take to bed should have a fascination with sex that goes beyond the physical. Think about it: During lovemaking, you literally put yourself inside another human being—giving you the opportunity to make a deep emotional connection with her as well. Every night doesn't have to be a tantric display of locked gazes and synchronized breathing, but at its best, it should feel as if we're doing something Zen, something divine, something extraplanetary.

For those intense moments, I should be all you're thinking about. On the most ecstatic nights of my life, I've been so focused on the man I was with that if the Rev. Al Sharpton had been next to us in bed, wrestling a 7-foot alligator, I would scarcely have noticed. A man who can say the same is truly one worth being naked with.

By the way, you're not the only one soaking the sheets. Women also have increased bloodflow to the genitals when they're sleeping. And in research from the Kinsey Institute, nearly 40 percent of women reported having an orgasm during a sex dream.

SEX IN FREUD'S CLOTHING

Dreams that aren't overtly sexual can sometimes have a sexual connotation. Example: You're in a fight, but your gun is too small or doesn't work. "You might be worried about your sexual potency or your creative power at work, in your family, or in society," says Bulkeley. "[We're] getting into Freudville here. Long, pointy objects—guns, swords, and tall buildings—often symbolize the male genitals, while hollow objects—purses, caves, boxes—often symbolize the female genitals. Bottom line: No object is always a genital symbol, but some often are."

Amazing Dream Fact

Men dream about strangers more often than women do. Women most often dream about people they know.

SEX SYMBOLS

Seemingly innocent dream images can actually have sexual connotations. That cute little kitty you dreamed about adopting? We doubt it's because you love cats.

> **FEMALE GENITALS:** cave, box, purse, cat, chick
>
> **MALE GENITALS:** gun, sword, missile, tall building
>
> **INTERCOURSE:** walking up stairs, opening a door, opening a box

Rated Rx

Clean out the mental clutter with some
of Hollywood's greatest hits.

BY RON GERACI

THE FORMER EDITOR of the *Saturday Review* was blessed by
a miracle 37 years ago: Watching Harpo Marx goose showgirls with a
bike horn saved his life.

When Norman Cousins was hospitalized with ankylosing
spondylitis—a debilitating arthritic disease that immobilizes you—
he decided he wasn't going to spend the last 6 months of his life
being prodded by box-shaped nurses in orthopedic shoes. Instead
he left the hospital and bunked down in a hotel, where he assem-
bled his own 1964 version of Comedy Central. He watched *Candid
Camera* and Marx Brothers films, laughed like an idiot, and—
despite his doctor's foretelling of a pine box—gradually recuper-
ated. In his 1979 memoir, *Anatomy of an Illness*, Cousins summed
it up: A funny movie is potent brain medication—one that can ease
pain, cure the body, and possibly send healing endorphins through
your veins.

The medicinal powers of great movies rival anything approved
by the FDA. Painkillers, amphetamines, tranquilizers, antidepressants, cinematic Viagra . . . they're all available for rent at $3 a dose.
But which movies can help you heal? Following are my personal cel-
luloid prescriptions for 26 common male ailments—flicks from the
doctor's bag of one cinemaphiliac.

BEST MOVIES TO CURE PREMARRIAGE COLD FEET

The nerve-racked state that arises from deliberating your next 50 years calls for a solid afternoon of film therapy. First watch *A New Leaf* (1971), with Walter Matthau. It's a classic comedy about an aging, destitute playboy who's desperate to marry a wealthy woman in 30 days. It'll let you see another guy who loves his freedom but is forced to consider shacking up because it'll be distinctly good for him. Second comes *Arthur* (1981), to let you conjure up your own fantasies of being the whim-driven, giggling drunk we'd all like to be, at least on weekends. Third is *Diner* (1982), for the contemplative gab on marrying another human being.

Notice there are no romantic kissy-screwy films here. You don't need movies that slap you in the head with potential rewards— that's why you proposed. You need to euthanize your fears about having sex with only one woman for the rest of your life. If those fears still linger after the above trilogy, add in *Birdman of Alcatraz* (1962) with Burt Lancaster; given an interesting subject, you'll have a universe to discover within your four walls. Then click on *Let It Be* (1970). If you think hanging with your buds for another 10 years will be as fun as it's always been, watch the Beatles bleed their death throes.

BEST MOVIE FOR SEDUCING YOUR WIFE

One of her romantic flicks will just highlight your shortcomings, and her aversion to even soft porn probably got you into this no-sex mess. So go under the radar. Rent *Yesterday, Today and Tomorrow*. In this 1963 Italian classic, Sophia Loren makes Tyra Banks look like Dog Chow. The striptease she does for Marcello Mastroianni is worth 10 porno tapes. The lust between the duo is infectious, which is why they made about 30 million films together. One of the film's vignettes explores the chore it can be to have a sexually insatiable wife, even if she's the number-one yank fantasy of men everywhere. That irony should jump-start light-hearted pillow talk on how much sex, at least for one of you, just ain't enough.

BEST MOVIE WHEN SOMEONE ELSE HAS SEDUCED YOUR WIFE

The Texas Chain Saw Massacre (1974) is tempting, but instead rent *Inferno*, a 3-D movie from 1953. (Or look for the 1973 TV remake, *Ordeal*, on cable.) A conniving wife conspires with her lover to leave her husband to die in the desert. Most men in his situation would become buzzard jerky. A few would not. Where do you fall?

BEST MOVIE WHEN YOU'VE SPROUTED A COLD SORE

Freaks (1932). The cast of heinously disfigured humans who could eat only by working in circus sideshows kept this fascinating film banned for decades. Most of these wretches lived lives collecting hurtful gawks and gasps from strangers afraid to come too close to them . . . and you can relate to that right now. As bad as it seems, your lip boil should be gone within 2 weeks—unlike that guy's coned skull.

BEST MOVIE FOR SEDUCING YOUR GIRLFRIEND

Push in a smoker to plant some filthy ideas, and the subliminal message—what have you got against five-on-one in the hot tub?—might have you staring at a locked front door. Better to attack her blind side by keeping it light. Throw some sexy stupidity in the VCR: Rent *Faster, Pussycat! Kill! Kill!*, a campy 1965 classic about three big-breasted broads who go on a violent tear in the desert. The shaking-camera breast shots and unapologetic corniness of the flick go down easy with white wine, and it'll encourage the type of silliness that eventually inspires flying panties.

BEST MOVIE FOR SEDUCING YOUR FRIEND, WHO'S A GIRL

If her IQ is above 70, don't invite her over to watch sap-fests like *When Harry Met Sally* (1989) or *Can't Buy Me Love* (1987); she'll see

through it. You might consider *Chasing Amy* (1997) if she's not a
woman who'll vomit during Ben Affleck's estrogen-curdling mono-
logue to Joey Lauren Adams. *Cape Fear* (1962) with Robert Mitchum
is a sneakier backup. This psycho-killer film sounds like a dusty classic
("Wait, you've never seen the original?"), but it'll have her wetting herself. Swoop in with the arm.

If, as is typical, she sees you as the sexless schmo next door who
holds no mystery, rent *City Lights* (1931). Read the box so you're familiar with the story. (Charlie Chaplin's little tramp falls in love with
a poor blind girl but is too ashamed to reveal his loser self to her.) Stay
quiet during the closing scene when the laughing, formerly blind girl
touches Chaplin's hands, at first dismissively, then with the excruci-
atingly slow, poignant realization of who he is. Rewind that scene and
play it again. Kiss her. If she doesn't kiss you back, she's unfit to bear
your children.

BEST MOVIE IF NONE OF YOUR SEDUCING HAS WORKED

Your VCR has already proved its value during dry spells. Now watch
a movie that doesn't require drawn shades, one that'll imbue you with
the right philosophy—*Pal Joey* (1957). It's Sinatra in the swinging '50s,
coming out of the worst years of his actual life, whistling from empty
taprooms to lonely hotels, all with an earned smirk that says, "If
nothing else, at least I get to hang around with me." Make that an appealing proposition. Read more. Run farther. Travel widely. You can
either bore yourself or sincerely enjoy your own company; both are
contagious.

BEST MOVIE AFTER GETTING DUMPED

The road from suicidal moaner back to vertebrate life has never
changed, but you can travel it 500 times and always forget the way.
Rerent *Swingers* (1996). But to see how it should be done, toss
Casablanca (1942) on the counter, too. Pretend it's an obscure flick

you've never heard of, one no one has ever recommended to you before. Tough guys cry, because they have to make tough choices. Meet Rick.

BEST MOVIE TO STICK IT TO YOUR EX

She wants to be friends? Invite her over and have *Titanic* (1997) cued to a few minutes before the ship crumbles in half. Click on the video and say, "Uh-oh, I forgot to return this" (after you watched it with whom, she'll ponder). As DiCaprio bites it and your ex is sappily wondering if anybody will ever love her that much, tenderly whisper, "On our happiest day, when everything was perfect . . . I still wouldn't have given up that hunk of wood for you." Watch expression change.

BEST MOVIE TO REGAIN MASCULINE DIGNITY AFTER 6 HOURS OF BRA SHOPPING

You're entitled to *Sorority Torture Chamber* and the unabridged Three Stooges collection, but grab *The Big Sleep* (1946). Bogey as detective Philip Marlowe and a hot-as-hell Bacall. The film oozes bull-milk straight through to the credits. Your penis will regain its lost half-inch by the second reel.

BEST MOVIE TO ENSURE THE WIFE MISSES YOU WHILE YOU'RE TRAVELING

Have her watch *Bad Ronald* (1974). Really, there's no psychotic teen living in the walls of your house. It's just a movie.

BEST MOVIE WHEN YOU NEED TO BULK UP

American Beauty (1999). Some regular sessions in the garage with dusty vinyl weights sent Kevin Spacey from a spaghetti-armed sofa slug to a man actually capable of taking his shirt off in public. It's the only believable thing in the movie for a reason: It's doable. Unlike Mena Suvari.

BEST MOVIE WHEN YOU NEED TO SLIM DOWN

Raging Bull (1980). Three hours of pugs bludgeoning each other will leave you with one take-home message: Lose 50 pounds, gain 50 pounds, whatever, it's a detail . . . one of the thousands of things you think is a huge, impossible mission that's actually just a series of small, simple decisions . . . the first of which involves the fries you're about to order.

BEST MOVIE WHEN YOU'RE HUNGOVER

Robin and the 7 Hoods (1964). You think you're hungover? You don't know crap about hungover. Crack an eye at Dino, Sammy, Bing, or Frank in this soft Alka-Seltzer farce. That's hungover. The rats moving slowly in big lapels, foghorning a few soothing songs, trying to remember the script, amusing themselves in what are supposed to be late 1920s Chicago speakeasies. It was the final gang movie for Sinatra and the guys (who lit up Vegas each night after filming), and something in their faces lets you know it. Maybe it's the bags under their smiling eyes. While you're holding the wet compress to your forehead and Dean is hurting right along with you, singing "Style," apply liberally the consoling salve of every earned morning after: Man, it was fun.

BEST MOVIE FOR INSOMNIA

Keep *JFK* (1991) cued to Donald Sutherland's "Mr. X" scene near the middle of the film, in which he mumbles to Costner on a park bench for what seems like 4 or 5 hours. It's video Xanax: a somnolent actor sleepwalking through a straw-voiced, muttered soliloquy while Oliver Stone's camera work does a slow fade to black. Set your TV timer to blink off at the end of this stultifying 17-minute scene; you'll likely conk out before the tube does. If not, watch it again. Charles Lindbergh couldn't have kept his eyes open through a second viewing.

BEST MOVIE TO HELP YOU CUT DOWN ON DRINKING

Avoid *Clean and Sober* (1988); Michael Keaton seems more talented drunk. Find *Come Fill the Cup* with James Cagney. He's an ex-newspaperman trying to shake booze back in 1951, before alcoholism became touchy-feely and anybody had ever heard of Betty Ford. When even a tough guy like Cagney can admit he needs to lay off the grape, demanding a little temperance in yourself puts you in fairly good company.

BEST MOVIE WHEN YOU'RE OVERWORKED

The Guns of Navarone (1961). Peck, Niven, and Quinn as commandos kicking fortified Third Reich butt. It's *Saving Private Ryan* (1998) without the crying or Ted Danson. You have a killer work schedule? Lick a pen and hit the to-do list.

BEST MOVIE WHEN YOU'RE UNAPPRECIATED

No promotion? Take in *The Shawshank Redemption* (1994). Maybe you feel like a chained monkey who's forced to do some bastard's bidding because somebody judged you wrongly. Andy, prisoner 37927, will tell you this: Mix a large dose of steady, diligent effort with a larger dose of patience, and comeuppances will follow for all who deserve them.

BEST MOVIE FOR FIRING SOMEONE

After you've completed the axing and you're miserable, soothe yourself by renting *The Last Survivors* (1975). After his passenger ship goes in the drink, Martin Sheen is the last officer alive on a hopelessly overcrowded lifeboat. He commences to decide who lives and who dies. Sheen's not a bad guy. He's just stuck in a bad situation with some bad choices to make.

BEST MOVIE AFTER TAKING THE BULLET YOURSELF

The film to watch if you were fired and need to crawl back from oblivion is *When We Were Kings* (1996). There are dozens of comeback films, but most of them will leave you wondering why Stallone let his career go to hell. This stylistic retro-documentary, set to B.B. King, paints the mood around a 1974 bout between an aging Muhammad

Ali and the younger, stronger, bigger George Foreman. The message: It's stupid not to be scared when everything's against you.

But it might come down to how long you can sweat it out in the jungle, and how many heart-exploding blows you can take before your demons momentarily get tired.

BEST MOVIES WHEN THE FLU HAS YOU FLAT ON YOUR BACK

Time is plentiful. First, watch *The Fly* (1986) and *Outbreak* (1995) to feel better about being conquered by an affliction that leaves you bereft of bodily control. Then pop some Rimantadine to *Rear Window* (1954), with James Stewart and Grace Kelly, and *Tattoo* (1981) with Bruce Dern and Maud Adams, to see how a guy can entertain himself while being cooped up in the house.

BEST MOVIES TO GET PSYCHED UP FOR A JOB INTERVIEW OR TO ASK FOR A RAISE

The quintessential rev-up flick is *Breaking Away* (1979). Catching a few minutes of those pumping 10-speeds will still make you want to sprint for the prize. Alternatively, fast-forward to the end of *Rocky* (the 1976 Oscar winner, not any of the asinine sequels). The sound-track crescendo during the climactic ring scene will leave you feeling unconquerable, mainly due to Bill Conti's "The Final Bell" cut, which sounds as powerful today as "Gonna Fly Now" does hokey. Start watching a few moments before Balboa is bashed to the mat, and his manager, Mick, pleads with him to stay down. Notice the un-blinking shock of the bald promoter with the cigar. Notice that there's not a single frame of idiotic slow motion. No cinematography has captured adrenaline better. And it has nothing to do with boxing. Anybody who expects a chump to show up in your shoes may have another think coming. And if you fail to land the job, con-sider this: Stallone's big break just set him up for a career of big dis-appointments.

BEST MOVIES TO BOND WITH YOUR SON

Apollo 13 (1995), *Fight Club* (1999), *Reservoir Dogs* (1992), or *Donnie Brasco* (1997). Mutually entertaining testosterone and plot situations that start the "What would you do?" rap. His answers will let you know him better, and you can give him your viewpoints on questions he'll never ask.

BEST MOVIES TO BOND WITH YOUR DAUGHTER

Go for offbeat comedies like *Waiting for Guffman* (1997), *Bread and Tulips* (2000), or *Amelie* (2001). Not only do you have a sensitive side, but you're deep enough to dig quirky films that make you think. You'll have something else to talk about, aside from her loser boyfriend.

BEST MOVIES TO PATCH THINGS UP WITH AN ANGRY, ESTRANGED SON OR DAUGHTER

Rent *Field of Dreams* (1989) or *National Velvet* (1944) if they're younger than 15 or a little slow. Otherwise, pick a film with a universal connecting point. *The Graduate* (1967) will subtly suggest that maybe even an old guy like you was once a confused schmuck in a world full of impatient manipulators. If the tension is too thick to sit still for an hour, have the Marx Brothers' *Animal Crackers* (1930) or *Duck Soup* (1933) at the ready—ancient, perfect comedies you can both digest with the same detached amazement.

BEST MOVIES FOR A MIDLIFE CRISIS

Rent *Cocoon* (1985) and *To Catch a Thief* (1955). You can be either a 51-year-old Wilford Brimley or a 51-year-old Cary Grant. The major difference is attitude—and the willingness to take steps two at a time. Hint: A 26-year-old Grace Kelly, with the sweetest bee-stung lips, wants to bang one of the above.

QUICKIES

YOUR LUCKY NIGHT

Anything can trigger it. A woman at the next table who's wearing a top that's revealing just enough skin, a coworker who's wearing the same scent your ex did, the picture of J.Lo you've taped inside your wallet to revisit every 10 minutes. Now it's in your head for good. You want sex. Tonight. But sex isn't like pizza; you can't feel a craving, start drooling, present a coupon, and expect it to be delivered to your door immediately. Too many factors are out of your control—namely, her desire and her urgency. So we asked a bunch of women to tell us the secret to guaranteed sex. Turns out, maybe the Domino's metaphor isn't far off. The advice: Just call ahead and place your order. Follow our minimal-effort suggestions and you'll be bed-bound—maybe not in 30 minutes, but surely by midnight.

To make sure she'll already be in the mood, simply jump-start her desire beforehand. "A really great thing you can do is to call her from a cell phone on your way home," says Ava Cadell, Ph.D., a California sexologist. "Tell her all the things you want to do with her, and how you've been fantasizing about your mouth on her and her mouth on you. Get her in the mood through the art of erotic communication. That way she's ready, and she's anticipating the excitement. Women need just a little bit of a production, and we need to be prepared." Dial now; operators are standing by. Here are some more tips from women on the receiving end.

Be Game

"When I come home and see Connect Four or Boggle on the dining-room table, I know what's on his mind. He knows my com-

petitive instincts lie very close to my sexual instincts, so that before
long we're the ones on top of the dining-room table, rolling the dice!"
says Adina, 27, of Santa Barbara, California.

Get on Her Page

"A text message on my cell phone would work for me. Those
seem sort of illicit to me, so he should send one that would make me
blush," says Tara, 27, of New York City.

Lay Down a Challenge

"A little reverse psychology works wonders on me. Like a message on my work voicemail saying, 'By the way, I was so not thinking
of you naked right now.' Or an e-mail that reads, 'Hey, hon, just
wanted to let you know that I have no intention of making you a
fabulous meal and then tackling you among the dirty dishes later
this evening, so see you later.' I guess it makes me want to change
his mind—or at least blow his mind," says Allegra, 32, of St. Louis,
Missouri.

Bribe Her

"I returned from a business trip at 10:30 P.M., and my boyfriend
had cleaned my apartment and left me a note on the newly cleaned
coffee table that said, 'Attention, Maura: There's a pasticcio in the
kitchen and ginger ale in the fridge. I hope you like it. I love you. See
you at 11:30. George.' An 'I love you' with a clean apartment and
some ready-to-eat Mediterranean cuisine always works for me!" says
Maura, 28, of New York City.

Play Dress-Up

"It always helps when he dresses up. Most of the time he tends
to look grungy in jeans and old T-shirts, but when he makes the effort
to spruce himself up for me—it makes me absolutely horny," says
Pam, 29, of Columbus, Ohio.

Get Naked

"The obvious works: like the time I walked in the door and various pieces of his clothing were shed on the way to the bedroom," says Judy, 28, of Princeton, New Jersey.

Convey Immediacy

"When my husband gives me a big, passionate kiss as I walk in the door, I'm in the mood immediately. It makes me feel as if he's been waiting to get his hands on me all day," says Christine, 26, of Chicago, Illinois.

GOOD CLEAN FUN

Like your sex hot 'n' steamy? Hit the showers!

Why is shower sex so much fun? First, "You're such a dirty girl" works as both valid excuse and kinky talk. Second, "the shower is basically a sex toy," says Anne Hooper, a sex therapist and author of *Great Sex Games*. "It combines heat, pressure, moisture, and friction, all in one device." It's even better than other sex toys because it doesn't require batteries, is self-cleaning, and is installed in nearly every living space and hotel room the world over. Of course, a shower stall in a luxury hotel is the most conducive venue for such slippery escapades, what with all those free soaps and lotions, big mirrors, and soundproof walls. But a humble at-home tub shower can work well, too, with a little care and a lot of hot water. You have the equipment; how you use it is up to you.

She'll surrender herself in the shower," says Yvonne K. Fulbright, a New York City sexologist. "There's something very releasing about water." To further enhance the molten mood, impress your shower companion with these H_2Orgasmic moves.

Mate on the Mat

Think safety before sex: Place a rubber mat on the shower floor to put your sexual contortions on a solid footing.

Scrub-a-Dub-Dub

Sensually scrub each other using body wash; it creates more suds and is easier to handle than soap. Try Philosophy Pumpkin Pie 3-in-1 shampoo, conditioner, and body-wash gel ($16, sephora.com). Pumpkin-pie scent significantly increases bloodflow to the penis, according to Alan Hirsch, M.D., director of the Smell and Taste Treatment and Research Foundation and author of *Scentsational Sex*.

Give Good Head

She'll love you nearly as much as her hairdresser if you massage her scalp. "Start with her shoulders, then knead her lower neck and work your way up to her scalp," suggests Fulbright. Try a shampoo with cucumber scent—like Ecoly Cucumber Shampoo ($12, ecoly.com)—which enhances female arousal, says Dr. Hirsch. Or try sex therapist Anne Hooper's suggestion and find an exotic scent like jasmine or patchouli, mentioned in the *Kama Sutra*.

Moisten Here

"A woman's natural lubrication will often be washed away in a shower, so many couples use a lubricant," says Wendy Fader, Ph.D., a psychologist and sex therapist. Without it, sex may be uncomfortable for her. Water-based lubes (such as Embrace or Astroglide) are fine in bed but won't hold up in water. Try a silicon-based lube (such as Eros or Body Action Xtreme).

INSTANT SEXPERT

What, Here?

Getting it on in a public place is a big taboo, which is why it's so much fun. According to a national survey of adults 18 to 65, parties are the most common communal location to have sex. The results, according to Adam & Eve, a dealer in erotica:

Party	32%
Movie	18%
Work	14%
Concert	7%
Wedding reception	6%

Wear a Life Jacket

Latex condoms can be used safely and effectively in water. You want a more secure fit than usual—look for "ultra-fit" on the label, says Adam Glickman, president of condomania.com. And put the condom on outside the shower to avoid getting water in it, which could cause slippage.

Testimonials from wet and happy women:

STEAMY APPEAL. "Sex in the shower is amazing. The heat relaxes your muscles, making it easier to get into fun positions. And candle-light through the steam gives a sensual glow," says Kristen, 29, a model.

MINTY FRESH. "I like to get my boyfriend really hard by using pep-permint soap on his penis. It makes his skin tingle," says Lisa, 27, a hat designer.

FULL PRESS. "It's amazing when my partner presses my breasts against the cold tile while entering me from behind; my whole body gets completely aroused," says Kristen.

THE DOWN-LOW. "I like going down on a man in the shower. It's such a turn-on when he's looking at me and water is running down his chest," says Michelle, 26, a cosmetics sales representative.

TRAVEL SHOWER. "My boyfriend and I have the best sex when we go out of town. Hotel showers are just more fun," says Veronica, 34, a jewelry designer.

STRIP TEST

We fell for breath strips when Listerine invented them; classier than gum, longer-lasting than drops, no rattling like Tic Tacs. Now every-body makes them. Our verdicts:

Wrigley's Eclipse Flash **** (out of four)
- In peppermint, spearmint, cinnamon.
- $1.50 for 24 strips

- Dissolves fast, lasts long, works well. Chills your mouth, throat, and sinuses. "Kiss me, you fool."

Winterfresh Thin Ice ***
- $1.50 for 24
- Dissolves slowly, brief licorice taste, powerful freshener. "It's Antarctica in your mouth!"

Listerine Pocketpaks **
- $2 for 24
- Dissolves quickly, very powerful, tingly but familiar. "Mouthwash, anyone?"

Myntz! Instastripz *
- "Cynnamon," "Peppermynt."
- $1.50 for 30
- Crumbles, sticks to the roof of your mouth. "No tyngle, breath still stynkz."

SEDUCTIONS

Stand up. Look down. You will see an appendage of amazing erotic ability dangling at waist level—your hand. Use it to massage your mate when she says she wants intimacy and doesn't necessarily mean sex. A massage is romance you can understand. It's practical. And it almost always leads to sex. Start with a good massage oil such as Neal's Yard Remedies Ginger & Juniper Warming Oil ($15 for 1.7 fluid ounces, nyr-usa.com) or Naturopathica Arnica Muscle and Joint Massage and Body Oil ($28 for 4 fluid ounces, naturopathica. com). Avoid mineral or baby oils because they are absorbed too quickly into the skin. Don't forget to rub your hands together to warm them before applying the massage oil and the following techniques:

1. Stroke toward the Heart
That means when you're working on her legs, stroke upward. On the arms, stroke downward.

2. Ease in with Effleurage

The French are experts at more than retreating. They know their massage. Effleurage is a simple stroke for loosening her up. It's a light, long, rhythmic stroke that generally runs with the grain of the muscle. On her legs, for example, use your cupped palms and gently glide upward. On her back, flatten your hands and broaden your strokes.

3. Play with Petrissage

This circular stroke is designed to squeeze the muscles and wring out tension from the shoulders, upper arms, legs, and buttocks. Use both hands to work the muscles in opposite directions: When stroking her thighs, for example, move one palm away from you as you slide it forward, and move the other toward you.

4. Roll Your Thumbs

This is best for working on tension knots. Use your thumbs, one after the other, to press into her flesh, sometimes moving circularly and other times just holding pressure on one point. Lean your weight into it.

ASK THE GIRL NEXT DOOR
The honest truth about women from our lovely neighbor

Phone Sex?

How do I keep a long-distance relationship hot?

—GEORGE, SAN FRANCISCO, CALIFORNIA

By switching to MCI, AT&T, or Verizon, depending on which is cheapest. An LDR (long-distance relationship) actually takes more effort and energy than a local love affair. Absence may make the heart grow fonder, but it tends to make women grow more paranoid about your feelings. Why? Simple: because they're not getting much in-the-flesh assurance of your commitment. So hour-long phone calls and frequent e-mails take on even greater importance. She needs to hear from you a lot. Bad news if she feels as if she's the one who's always calling. Think of an LDR as a campfire. If you don't tend to it constantly, the flame goes out—and leaves you cold.

Aural Sex

Sometimes my girlfriend screams, sometimes she moans, and other times she barely makes any noise. Are orgasms really that different?
—G.S., DUNCANVILLE, TEXAS

Yeah. Orgasms are a little like sneezes. There are the big, intense, explosive ones that send a girl's entire body into an involuntary spasm. Then there are small ones that barely register but are still quite nice. There's the kind we . . . know . . . are . . . coming . . . any . . . second—and those that we think are going to happen and then don't (but then happen later and are extra-good). And, of course, there are the orgasms that take us completely by surprise (my favorite). Each type of orgasm might elicit a different sound. But there's another factor at work: mood. Whether your girlfriend screams, moans, whimpers, or stays silent when she peaks probably depends a lot on her frame of mind. Like all women, she's bound to feel quiet and sleepy some nights, and rowdy and raunchy on others. Bottom line: As long as she doesn't shout some other guy's name, it's all good.

Ex Marks the Spot

Do women ever fantasize about their ex when they're in bed with their current guy? —ANONYMOUS

No. The time a woman might fantasize about her ex is while masturbating, when she's envisioning reruns of the greatest moments in her sexual history. Typically, when we're really into a new guy, we can't help thinking about him all the time, and he takes the leading role in all our fantasies (except those starring Brad Pitt). In fact, once a woman is in a new relationship with a man she really cares about, she quickly forgets about her ex altogether.

Your Prayers Have Been Answered

Do straight women ever fantasize about other women?

—MIKE C., STEAMBOAT SPRINGS, COLORADO

Yes, although most women I know feel kind of funny about it afterward. We don't picture anything as *Playboy*-esque as Angelina Jolie covered in whipped cream (although I just did). It's more like fantasizing about a woman as part of an attractive couple—or a threesome, depending on our mood—going at it. Hmm, how can I best explain? You know your favorite scene in *Mulholland Drive*? Well, that turns us on, too.

A beautiful woman is just as beautiful in a woman's eyes as in a man's. And fantasizing about a woman feels a little deviant and naughty, which makes it a hot addition to our visions. I've also heard women confess that they sometimes imagine what it would be like to fool around with one of their sexier female friends. I've tried to do that before, but find it's much easier to picture strangers getting kinky than women I know well. When I conjure up a friend's face in ecstasy, she immediately raises her fantasy eyebrow and asks me, "What the hell are you doing?"

Heel, Boy
Do women like having sex doggy-style?   —BENNY, BY E-MAIL

Yes, we like it. A lot of women love it. But unless you're dating a woman who likes to refer to herself as your bitch, I wouldn't advise calling it "doggy-style." If you absolutely have to describe it, call it having sex "from behind." It can be very stimulating to her G-spot, if she's into that. Your best option for repeat performances is not to call it anything. Just do it.

For more honest answers about women, look for Ask the Men's Health Girl Next Door *wherever books are sold.*

INDEX